THE SIGNS OF OUR TIMES

THE SIGNS OF OUR TIMES

12 BIBLICAL REASONS WHY THIS COULD BE THE GENERATION OF THE RAPTURE

MICHAEL SAWDY

**BIBLICAL SIGNS
PUBLISHING**

Published in Plymouth, Michigan, by Biblical Signs Publishing, an imprint of BiblicalSigns.com.

This Book may be purchased in bulk for educational, business, fund-raising, or sales promotional use. For information, please email BiblicalSigns@gmail.com.

Unless otherwise noted, Scripture quotations in this book are taken from the King James Version. Public domain.

All italics in Scripture quotations were added by the author for emphasis.

ISBN 978-0692144879

Library of Congress Control Number: 2018907795

Cover Design by MichaEL Sawdy.

Printed in the United States of America

TO GOD:

The website and this book would not have been possible without Your unwavering mercy, grace, love, faithfulness, and the guidance of Your Holy Spirit - Who never fails to inspire me. Thank You for everything.

TO MOM:

Thank you for always being there, especially back in the days when I wasn't worth being there for. If not for your prayers and faithfulness, as a Godly mother, I would not be around to write this book today. This book is, no doubt, a testament to your Proverbs 22:6 parenting. I will always love you more than my own life itself.

TO DAD:

Thank you for being there whenever I call on you. You are truly an example of what a Godly father and man should be. Though I was a problem child growing up, you made sure that you coupled love with your discipline. Both have made me the man that I have become today. I am eternally thankful to call you my Dad.

TO BRO:

Though we had fought and argued like cats and dogs growing up, we never let that affect our brotherly love. I'm so happy that you didn't follow in my early footsteps of life, but that you took lessons from the consequences of my many mistakes and charted your own path. I'm so glad that you have drawn closer to the Lord in recent years, and I pray that He will bring you closer to Him each new day - as He has me. Love ya' Bro!

TO FAMILY:

I could not have asked for a better family. I've been blessed by the wisdom of Uncle Jim, Grampa, Uncle Jerry, and Uncle Butch. Aunt Pam, you share my strong faith in God's Word and His Light radiates through you to the entire family. Gramma and Aunt Deb, I'm beyond grateful for your gentle love since the day I was born. Aunt Jude, Tommy, Dawn, Uncle Pat, Uncle Ray, Cindy, Sarah, and Chris S, I'm blessed to have every one of you in my life. Kendall & Kaylee, never forget that God is always there for you when you need Him - as am I. God bless you all. I love you all.

CONTENTS

INTRODUCTION

THE DISCIPLES SAID UNTO JESUS, TELL US... WHAT SHALL BE
THE SIGN OF THY COMING, AND OF THE END OF THE AGE?

- MATTHEW 24:3

THIS WAS THE MILLION-DOLLAR question that was posed to
Lord Jesus by His disciples in Matthew 24:3. I suspect they had
no idea that His answer would be referring to events set to take
place thousands of years in the future. They'd probably assumed
that after He died on the Cross, rose from the dead, and ascended
into Heaven, that He'd come right back down - so that the Golden
Age of their Messianic King could begin. They were unaware, at
that time, that He was not only coming to be the Messiah of the
Jews - but the Saviour of *all* mankind. They didn't realize that the
Father in Heaven sent Jesus to reconcile the *entire* sinful human
race unto Himself.

While I believe they perceived Jesus' death and Resurrection
as the end of the world as they'd known it, and the dawn of their
Messiah's reign on Earth, Jesus was indeed preparing to usher in
a new age - just not the one they were expecting. It would become
what we now know as the Age of Grace. This is the age in which
we currently live. It's the age in which all human beings (Jew and
Gentile alike) can repent of their sins, get washed of their sins in
Christ's atoning blood, and be reconciled unto our Holy God and
Father in Heaven (YHWH).

9

Until our Lord comes again, every man and woman on Planet Earth can begin a relationship with their Creator - through Christ. Though once He returns, the Age of Grace abruptly ends. So, my advice to everyone reading this is to get right with God while the gift of grace is freely given (Ephesians 2:8). Otherwise, if you do not accept Him as the Saviour of your soul in this age, you'll be destined to meet Him as the Just Judge when He returns.

Getting back to His disciples' question... what will the sign of His (second) coming to Earth be, and of the end of the age? Jesus went into great detail to explain what the "Last Days" generation would need to look for. He gave many signs. You will be excited to know that *our generation* is the first in history to ever see *every sign* (pre-Tribulation) that Christ gave being fulfilled. While there have been numerous generations of Christians who believed that they were *the* generation, this book explains why certain essential signs are exclusive only to our day. I'll delve into, what I believe to be, twelve of the biggest signs. Most were given by Lord Jesus in Matthew 24 and Luke 21. I also chose others from elsewhere in the Bible, because they are far too prevalent today to not address.

All of the signs you will read about herald our Lord's Second Coming, so you may be wondering why I subtitled the book: *The Generation of the Rapture* - not The Generation of *His Return*? Because Jesus' return occurs *after* the seven-year Tribulation that is described in the Book of Revelation. The Rapture (described in 1st Thessalonians 4:16-18) is the event that evacuates us believers *out of* this world *before* the Tribulation begins (Revelation 3:10). So, it's definitely something we should all be looking forward to! By the time you are done reading this book (believer or not), you will be looking up to the skies a whole lot more. Like me, you're going to strongly believe that the Rapture of the faithful and the return of Jesus Christ are so truly "*at the doors*" (Matthew 24:33).

CHAPTER ONE

ANTI-SEMITISM

JESUS SAID, THE TIME COMETH, THAT WHOSOEVER KILLETH
YOU (JEWS) WILL THINK THAT HE DOETH GOD SERVICE. AND
THESE THINGS WILL THEY DO UNTO YOU, BECAUSE THEY
HAVE NOT KNOWN THE FATHER, NOR ME.

- JOHN 16:2-3

GOD LOVES THE JEW. From the beginning, He always has, still does, and always will. You cannot study the entirety of the Bible and come to any other conclusion. Jesus Christ, who was God in the flesh, came down to Earth *as a Jew*.

As believers, we are called to love what God loves and to hate what He hates. On the flipside, Satan has always loved what God hates and has hated - with a passion - that which the LORD loves. Thus it is no wonder that in this world, which is under the control of the devil (John 12:31, 2nd Corinthians 4:4, 1st John 5:19), the Jewish people have always been the most hated and persecuted race in the history of mankind. There are countless examples in the Bible, and all throughout history, of demonic leaders or even entire nations coming against the Jews to destroy them. We read of the devil's first stance against the Jewish Nation, Israel, in 1st Chronicles 21:1 - "Satan stood up *against* Israel."

Since that time, the devil has influenced many wicked men in positions of power, from every generation, to attempt to eradicate

Israel and the Jewish people from the Earth. The Book of Esther speaks of the wicked Persian named Haman. He was the Hitler of Biblical times. He sought to destroy all the Jews (Esther 3:6-14). Thankfully, he did not succeed in his quest. Rather, God turned the wicked device of Haman back upon his own head - *literally*. He and his sons were hung on the very same gallows that Haman had prepared for the Jews (Esther 9:1-5). Whenever Satan thinks he has the Jewish people right where he wants them, preparing to annihilate them, Almighty God flips the script.

Throughout history, anyone who's ever sought to destroy the Jews has instead been destroyed themself. Every nation that has ever tried to enslave or to kill off their race is no longer a global power. Today, Egypt is just a strip of land among many nations in the Middle East. Babylon is gone. Greece and Rome are shells of their former selves. And when's the last time that any of you have met a real Nazi? I'm not talking about a skinhead teenager who is confused and mad at the world. No... I mean a living breathing member of the Nazi Party? You have not, and you won't, because they're long gone. Hitler's territory has today become 35 separate European countries, and his Nazis are non-existent.

Meanwhile, the Jews have miraculously survived and outlived every powerful empire that has ever sought to exterminate them. While Adolf Hitler and his regime murdered 6-million Jews, they could not put an end to the age-old race of Hebrews. Instead, the Jewish people (well over 6-million of them) are back today where they have always belonged - in their Biblical Promised Land of Israel. Hitler and his Nazis are defunct. Why do you think that is? How is that possible? The answer is simple and short: GOD. He has stated so many times, in His Word, that He'll curse those who curse the Jews and all those attempting to wipe them out will be wiped out themselves. Still, many men have believed Satan's lies.

They believed that God was done with the Jewish people and Israel, as so many ignorant people still believe in our day and age.

Satan is the father of lies, and he will continue to incite hatred and animosity toward the Jews until Christ returns to put an end to him - and his lies - once and for all. One of the most successful lies Satan has ever told is that "the Jews killed Jesus." Hitler used this falsehood to propel himself to power. Sadly, most Christians followed him because of this great deception. The truth is that a tiny group of powerful and corrupt Jews of the Scribes, Pharisees, and Sadducees, were behind the torture and crucifixion of Jesus - not every Jew who has ever lived!

Not even every member of those cliques of "holy" men were against Jesus. Men such as Nicodemus, Joseph of Arimathea, and even Saint Paul had belonged to those Councils of Jewish priests. It was the top brass of the Councils who'd really "killed Jesus," along with the turncoat disciple (Judas Iscariot) and the Romans. Still, Satan has deceived many to believe that because *some* Jews played a part then *all* Jews must be guilty. The truth is, as I stated earlier, *Jesus Christ was a Jew*. All of His twelve disciples were *Jews*, along with 99% of His first followers. Every Book in our Bible, with the exception of just two, was written by a *Jew*. There are 66 books in the Word of God we hold today, meaning that 64 of those were penned by *Jews*.

How could all of the wonderful things that you've read about Jesus (which led you to become a Christian in the first place) have been penned by someone who had taken part in murdering Jesus? It doesn't make much sense, does it? None of Satan's lies ever do. Lord Jesus loves His Jewish brethren with the same undying love that His Father in Heaven has for them, as He and Father YHWH are *"One"* (John 10:30). The main reason He comes back down is to save Israel from certain destruction by their many enemies who come against them in the Latter Days. If He loves the Jews and Israel so much, to make His Second Coming all about defending them, then why are some Christians anti-Semites? Apparently, it's because a lot of believers today just don't know their Holy Bibles.

You can't call yourself a Christian, while holding anti-Semitic views. Christianity and anti-Semitism are antithetical. If you are harboring hatred toward the Jewish people, then you are standing with the devil. Like it or not, it's Bible truth. Genuine Christianity has never taught nor endorsed anti-Semitism of any kind, but that has not stopped wicked men from twisting and perverting God's Word to make it appear so. The Apostle Paul was actually given foreknowledge that some people (even Christians) would attempt to do this. Paul cautioned against believers in Christ becoming too haughty toward the Jews and Israel. He said that there would even be some who would proclaim that God was *done* with the Jewish people, or preach that the Church has become the *new* Israel.

In Romans, Chapter 11, he rebuked anyone who'd teach such nonsense. He said, in verses 1 and 2 -

"HATH GOD CAST AWAY HIS PEOPLE? GOD FORBID. FOR I ALSO AM AN ISRAELITE, OF THE SEED OF ABRAHAM, OF THE TRIBE OF BENJAMIN. GOD HATH NOT CAST AWAY HIS PEOPLE WHICH HE FOREKNEW."

Paul went on to explain that we Christians are "grafted into" God's chosen Family Tree after we put our faith in Jesus Christ, but that we by no means *replace* the Jews. He said that if we were to ever "boast" against Israel or the Jewish people, implying that God was done with them, then God would be *done with us*. So, if anyone ever tries to feed you the demonic lie that Israel and the Jews mean nothing to God anymore, refer them to that powerful Chapter of Romans. If anti-Semitic Christians continue believing and teaching that false doctrine, then they do so at their own peril.

Sadly, most early Church leaders and Popes were Jew-haters. Many engaged in systematic discrimination against the Jews, and that led to persecution - which led to expulsion and exile - which ultimately led to execution. Prepare to be just as shocked as I was when you read some of these well-known names. First, there was

Constantine. Between the years 315 and 337 AD, he had enacted harsh laws targeting the Jews. Then, there's John Chrysostom of Antioch, the Archbishop of Constantinople. He was definitely not the great "doctor of the Church" which he is revered as today. His views and teachings on Jews (or "Judaizers," as he'd called them) do not reflect the doctrine of the Bible in any way, shape, or form.

Popular saints in Catholicism, such as Origen and Augustine, published what many consider to be anti-Semitic writings. Also, a majority of Popes throughout the centuries of the early Catholic Church were aggressively anti-Semitic. Some of them had called for Jews to be expelled from nations, and to even be put to death. Now, I don't want Catholics reading this to get the idea that this is an attack on the Catholic Church - because it is not. It is simply historical truth that needs to be told.

Martin Luther, the trailblazing reformer who'd broken away from Catholicism to form Protestantism, left the Church of Rome because of disagreements he had with their authority - especially regarding the Vatican's anti-Semitism. Unfortunately, later in life, when he could not convert as many Jews to Christianity as he had hoped, disappointment turned into hatred. His later writings were very hostile toward the Jewish people.

There are many today who do not want to believe this, but his material is available for anyone to examine. Luther published *On the Jews and Their Lies* in 1543. In the pamphlet, he advocates an 8-point plan to "get rid of" the Jews as a distinct group through religious conversion or by expulsion. Some of the worst language reads, "set fire to their synagogues or schools" and "their houses should be razed and destroyed." It is extremely sad that someone like him can be so revered today. Yes, times were different back then; and some say that with Him being raised in an anti-Semitic church, it was inevitable that he would develop such views. Still, for someone with such supposed knowledge of the Word of God, there is no excuse. He should have known better!

15

Another widely-revered religious figure who taught that God was done with the Jewish people was Muhammad, the author of Islam. A majority of Muslims hold anti-Semitic beliefs, because the unholy Quran teaches them to hate the Jews. Islam's so-called "prophet" once watched as many as 600 Jews being beheaded in Medina in one day. Allah's word instructs Muslims to "*slay the Jew* wherever you find them."

Don't believe the lie that Muslims only burn the Israeli flags because they "don't like Zionists," and not because it is a Jewish symbol. The truth is that whenever they use the words "Death to Israel" or "Kill the Zionists," every Muslim on Earth knows that these phrases are code for "Kill the Jews." They simply substitute "Zionists" for "Jews" so they can openly express their unbridled anti-Semitism publicly, without receiving the condemnation for it. Anti-Zionism *is* anti-Semitism, no matter what they say.

It irritates me when I hear anti-Semitic Muslims crying about prejudice or discrimination against Islam. Many call us Christians "Islamophobic" or "intolerant." Well, they're actually right on one count, because I will *never* "tolerate" a religion whose creed is to "Destroy Israel and the Jews." Muslims won't receive one shred of sympathy from me, as to how they are treated, until they learn to treat the Jewish people and the Jewish State with respect.

They have turned a term that God loves into a dirty word in our generation. I am sure that you have all heard the Muslims and conspiracy theorists call the Jews "Zionists." The term does not mean whatever they want you to think that it means. In reality, a Zionist is someone who believes the Biblical promises of God to return the Jewish people back to their ancient Homeland of Israel. I believe that. So, that makes *me* a Zionist. Many Christians today are Zionists - not just Jews and Israelis. I'd hope everyone reading this book is a Zionist!

Unfortunately, youth today have been programmed to believe that Zionists are "bad people." Does that make me a bad person?

Am I part of some global Zionist conspiracy? Nope. I'm simply doing my best to live according to God's Will in this life; and His Will (for everyone) is to love, support, and defend Israel. Sad to say, today's younger generation are doing the complete opposite. Due to enemies of the Jews flooding social media platforms with anti-Israel propaganda, one recent study found that anti-Semitism has skyrocketed about 50% on America's college campuses.

By far, the number one contributor to the rise of Jew-hatred in American universities is the anti-Israel *Boycott, Divestment, and Sanctions* movement. The BDS is an Islamist-inspired campaign against the Jewish State that has led to Nazi swastikas on doors of Jewish students, along with messages such as "Hitler did nothing wrong." Some faculty members make anti-Semitic gestures in the classrooms, and Stars of David with an "X" scratched into them appear on walls, windows, and doors. At rallies, BDS supporters hand out materials that deny the Holocaust, and promote attacks against Jews and "Jew-lovers." BDS'ers protest, harass, or disrupt pro-Israel speakers - sometimes preventing lectures altogether.

While Muslim hatred of Israel dates back about 1,500 years, BDS was started in 2005 by Omar Barghouti. Barghouti has made no bones about the goal of BDS being "the destruction of Israel." Most people today don't realize that Islamic nations were Hitler's greatest allies in his quest to "exterminate" the Jews. The Jewish people were expelled by decree from all Islamic lands and thrown out of many European countries - Spain, France, Italy, England, Russia, Poland, Portugal, and (of course) Germany.

Not long after Adolf Hitler published his grossly anti-Semitic book, *Mein Kampf,* in 1925, he'd become the ruthless dictator of Germany. Between 1939-1945, He devised the "final solution" to eradicate the Jews, culminating in the tragic Holocaust. Between 1933-1941, persecution of the Jews in Germany rose rapidly until they had been stripped of their rights - not only as citizens, but as human beings. Anti-Semitism had reached an all-time high under

Adolf Hitler's Nazi Party rule. In 1938, the deportations of Jews to concentration camps (and ultimately the gas chambers) began.

It has been recorded that when trains bound for gas chambers (filled with screaming Jews) would pass by German churches, the congregations would play their music louder so they could drown out the horrific cries for help. This is one of the most disgusting things that I have ever heard in my life. Due to intimidation by the Nazis, most Christians had remained silent during the systematic murder of God's chosen people. With the exception of a handful of courageous believers, like Dietrich Bonhoeffer, the majority of Christendom in Europe stood by and watched as 6-million Jews perished. This, in my opinion, is the greatest stain on Christianity in history. Bonhoeffer was a fearless German pastor who opposed Hitler, and preached the wise words -

"SILENCE IN THE FACE OF EVIL IS ITSELF EVIL. GOD WILL NOT HOLD US GUILTLESS. NOT TO SPEAK IS TO SPEAK. NOT TO ACT IS TO ACT."

Amen. In 1945, he was hung by Hitler for publicly speaking out against the Nazi regime. Bonhoeffer is an inspiration and role model for all believers. As anti-Semitism is again rearing its ugly head in our generation, we must not be afraid to speak out loudly against it. Whether on social media or television, in schools or the public square, the lies and blood libels against the Jewish people and Israel cannot be tolerated! Christians must strongly refute and condemn them. It does not take long in our society for rumours or trends to spread like wildfire, and kids today will follow whatever is "trending" in their world. Germany has proved it only takes one popular voice to gain the ear of an entire nation. Just imagine if Hitler had Twitter at his disposal!

If anti-Semitism were to gain a foothold amongst the youth of this generation, I shudder to think how rapidly it would spread.

Take a look at Europe... as more Muslims have migrated there, anti-Semitism has shot through the roof. Jews are fleeing Europe in droves. An eye-opening study by the Anti-Defamation League (ADL) revealed 25% of the world - more than *one-billion* people - hold anti-Semitic views. 1/4 of the globe hates the Jew! What can those of us who love God's precious people do about such troubling statistics? We must always remember that the Holocaust happened because virtually all Christians back then did *nothing*. We cannot remain silent like believers of Hitler's day had done.

If the Jews look to anyone for protection in this evil world, it should be us Christians. We are called by God to be their greatest ally. It is our duty to defend them, because *their* greatest enemy is *our* greatest enemy. That enemy, of course, is Satan. The devil's been targeting God's chosen from the very beginning. When he becomes too frustrated with not being able to destroy the Jewish people, be sure he will come for us Christians next. If you haven't been paying attention, he has already begun to.

THE LORD SAID, I WILL BLESS THEM THAT BLESS THEE (JEWS), AND CURSE HIM THAT CURSETH THEE: AND IN THEE SHALL ALL FAMILIES OF THE EARTH BE BLESSED.

- GENESIS 12:3

CHAPTER TWO

CHRISTIAN PERSECUTION

JESUS SAID, THEN SHALL THEY DELIVER YOU UP TO BE
AFFLICTED, AND SHALL KILL YOU: AND YE SHALL BE HATED
OF ALL NATIONS FOR MY NAME'S SAKE.

- MATTHEW 24:9

2018'S WORLD WATCH LIST, an annual report released by the Christian persecution watchdog group Open Doors USA, revealed that one out of every twelve Christians globally lives in an area where there is high-level persecution. There are over 200-million Christians who are living in areas of the world where our Faith is illegal, forbidden, or punished. Open Doors tracks and monitors reports of Christian persecution around the world, and then ranks the 50 countries which are the biggest offenders.

Last year, over 3,000 believers had been murdered, more than 1,200 were kidnapped, about 800 churches were vandalized, and over 1,000 Christian women were raped or sexually harassed. In this world, every day, about a half-dozen women are being raped, sexually abused, or forced into Muslim marriages under the threat of death for their faith. There were at least 15 Christian teenagers kidnapped and forced into Islamic marriages in 2017 alone. Open Doors' report had revealed that Islamism is still the main driver of

Christian persecution globally. Muslim-majority nations account for 36 of the list's 50 countries.

While North Korea topped the list, for the 16th year in a row, Afghanistan had given the oppressive atheist country a run for its money. Along with Afghanistan, there were many other countries that had witnessed a dramatic rise in incidents last year. The most notable among them were Egypt, India, Libya, and Turkey. Egypt has been moving up the list rapidly, due to hundreds of heinous attacks on the Christian community in recent years.

Two years ago, in 2016, a Muslim mob in Cairo had stripped down an elderly Christian woman and paraded her naked on the streets. This occurred during an attack in which seven Christian homes had been looted and torched. The attack, in the village of Karma, began after rumors spread that the old woman's Christian son had relations with a Muslim girl. Egypt's top Christian cleric said that the 70-year-old woman was dragged out of her home by the mob, who'd beat her and insulted her, before stripping off her clothes. As they forced her to walk through the streets nude, they chanted "Allahu Akbar" (which means "Allah is great"). In Islam, Muslim women are forbidden to marry Christian and Jewish men. Yet, Muslim men are permitted to marry Christian women.

In 2011, many churches had been set on fire in Egypt during a national uprising. In another instance of a Muslim woman being romantically involved with a Christian man, an Islamic mob had burned the church of the man. Large groups of Coptic Christians filled the streets to protest the church being burned. The Egyptian army arrived to stop the protests, and killed 25. That tragic event became known as the "Maspero Massacre." The Copts had been met with riot police and tanks. As the army vehicles charged at protesters, at least six were crushed under the tanks.

There has also been a wave of kidnappings in Egypt, in which young Christian girls are being abducted and forced into Islamic marriages. The girls (as young as 15) are snatched from homes, schools, and sidewalks, by Muslim men who forcibly take them as wives. Families of the abducted girls have begged the police authorities for help, but to no avail. The crimes have been taking place under the radar in Egypt for about 50 years. In the province of Qena, there were nearly 75 reported kidnappings and reports of violence against the Copts from 2011-2014. Since the authorities investigating the crimes are Muslim, virtually none of the missing girls have been returned to their families.

In 2017, during "Easter" celebrations, Islamists bombed two Egyptian churches - murdering nearly 50 believers. Four months earlier, at Christmastime, about 30 Christians had been murdered when Islamic terrorists bombed the main cathedral in Cairo. The Islamists love to carry out large-scale attacks on major Christian or Jewish Holidays. They also commit scores of attacks against us "infidels" during their "holy" days. On the first day of the Islamic month of Ramadan in 2017, followers of the so-called *religion of peace* murdered over two-dozen churchgoers. 28 Christians lost their lives in that attack, and another 25 were wounded.

A bus was traveling to a church south of Cairo, when three four-wheel drive vehicles pulled up alongside it and opened fire. When the bus came to a stop, ten gunmen wearing fatigues and masks exited their vehicles and then approached passengers that remained alive. Next, came the life or death question...

"Are you Christian?"

When the passengers answered, "Yes," the Islamic terrorists distributed a pamphlet unto them which contained Quranic verses explaining Ramadan. The attackers then ordered the Christians to recite the Shahada from the pamphlet - the Muslim profession of faith. When our brothers and sisters in Christ refused and said, "No. We were born Christian and will die Christian," the terrorists opened fire at close range and murdered those refusing to convert.

Coptic Christians only make up 10% of Egypt's population of 92-million - apparently 10% *too many* for the Islamic nationalists. The Muslims murdering Christians in Islamic nations are not all members of terror groups like ISIS either. Rather, they are regular everyday adherents of Islam. Their "holy book" instructs them to strike terror in the hearts of unbelievers (us Christians and Jews), and to "slay" us wherever they find us. Any Christian who says "we are all children of God," and "Islam is a religion of peace," needs to say those words while looking into the eyes of a Coptic Christian. It is my opinion that the Copts would strongly disagree.

9 out of the Top 10 worst countries for Christians to live are Islamic nations. Those nations are Afghanistan, Somalia, Sudan, Pakistan, Eritrea, Libya, Iraq, Yemen, and Iran. While the African nations of Nigeria, Ethiopia, Kenya, and Central African Republic are not Muslim-majority (like much of the continent), that hasn't stopped Islamist groups from bringing their oppression and terror to Christians in those nations too. Asian nations like Malaysia, the Philippines, Indonesia, and the Maldives show that persecution of believers by Islamists is not exclusive to the Middle East.

Also in Asia, there is another alarming form of persecution - and that is government-led persecution. The number one offender in this category, and the number one most dangerous country in the world for a Christian to live, is North Korea. Public worship is forbidden there. The Christian population, of around 300,000, are forced to hide beliefs or fellowship. At least 50,000 Christians are wasting away in prison or labor camps for their faith.

ODUSA says "it is illegal to be a Christian in North Korea," and believers are often sent to labor camps or are killed if they are discovered. You'd be arrested for carrying a Bible on the streets of North Korea, and for simply saying "God bless you" or "Merry Christmas." Believers who have been fortunate enough to escape the hell of living under Kim Jong Un's atheist regime give horrific accounts of forced starvation or abortions, crucifixion of believers over fires, and Christians being crushed under steamrollers.

There's another government-led persecutor in the Asia region who should be higher on the list, and that is China. The Chinese government regularly orders demolition of churches, because they perceive Christianity to be a threat to the Communist government. Some believers there are ordered to remove images of Lord Jesus, and to replace them with pictures of President Xi Jinping. This year, Xi cemented his position as China's dictator - possibly for life. The Chinese parliament voted to eliminate the term limit for the Presidency, paving the way for Xi to serve indefinitely.

Spokesmen for the President issue statements you'd expect to hear in an End Times film about Antichrist. One of Xi's officials, Qi Yan, has said, "Many rural people are ignorant… thinking God is their Savior. After our cadres' work, they will come to realize their mistakes and will think: we should no longer rely on Jesus, but on the party for help." Another official that's close to Xi made a similar statement, saying, "Christians are ignorant, and need to be taught to worship the state - not God."

Under the leadership of Xi, thousands of Crosses have been forcibly removed from churches, hundreds of churches have been destroyed, pastors and priests have been arrested, and the Bible's even been *banned*. In early 2018, Chinese Christians were unable to find the Bible listed on their country's biggest retail websites. According to *South China Morning Post*, searches for "Bible" on Amazon, Taobao, Jingdong, or Dang Dang, yielded a "no results" response. Search analytics revealed a large spike in the keyword "Bible" on March 30th; but two days later, the analytics showed 0 searches. The data proved that the government began censoring the word on the internet.

Before being banned online, the Holy Bible was prohibited in China's commercial brick-and-mortar stores. It was only available for purchase in church bookstores. Texts of all other major Faiths, such as Buddhism, Islam, Hinduism, and Taoism are available to purchase in Chinese stores and online. An atheist blogger for the *Patheos* website actually took issue with the Bible ban, writing, "The Chinese policy just adds fuel to the Christians' persecution complex, and no one can say that, in this case, they don't have a valid, even important point."

One of the most surprising countries on the World Watch List would have to be India. I'm sure many think, as I once did, that India is made up primarily of hippie Buddhists and Hindus. That is not the case. In recent years, a very disturbing trend has been forming in the Hindu and Buddhist nations – *radicalism*. Hindu nationalism has rapidly spread across India since the election of Prime Minister Narendra Modi. Under Modi, religious freedom violations against Christians have spread unchecked. Last year, Open Doors documented 600+ persecution incidents; but said that most cases remain unreported, so the true number is much higher.

Next door to India, Hindu-majority Nepal has criminalized conversion to Christianity or Judaism. Buddhist nationalism has led to a dramatic and violent rise in hostility toward Christians in the countries of Sri Lanka, Bhutan, and Myanmar.

2018 was the 26th year that Open Doors USA published the World Watch List. Over the past 25 years, just three countries have ever topped the list: North Korea (2002-2017), Saudi Arabia (1993-1995, 1998-2001), and Somalia (1996-1997). The Top Ten nations over the 25-year span were North Korea, Saudi Arabia, Iran, Somalia, Afghanistan, Maldives, Yemen, Sudan, Vietnam, and China. These nations fulfill Philippians 3:18, being "enemies of the Cross of Christ."

A three-year research study, reported in 2016 and conducted by an International Catholic Charity (Aid to the Church in Need), found that Christians comprised 75% of those persecuted for their religion globally. The study revealed that Christians are not only more persecuted than any other Faith group, but that they are also experiencing the very worst forms of persecution. Christians have been martyred for their beliefs more so than any other Faith group over the past two decades. In 2016 alone, a follower of Christ was murdered for their beliefs *every 6 minutes*.

In the Middle East region, the only safe haven for believers is the Holy Land of Israel. While the Western world has not yet seen persecution of Christians reach the violent levels of the Mideast or Asia, I believe we're leaning in that dangerous direction more and more each and every new year. During the administration of Barack Obama, especially following the Supreme Court decision to essentially legalize same-sex marriage nationwide, Americans holding the Biblical worldview were under attack. Believers were taken before courts or fined, fired from jobs, had their businesses shut down, and were even *imprisoned*. What was the crime? Only refusing to violate their deeply held Faith.

In the minds of liberal Americans today, Freedom of Speech and Expression should apply to everyone *except* Christians. When we publicly express our Faith, and take a stand against something which the Bible has deemed immoral, we're told to shut up or are shouted down as hateful bigots. Yet, whenever someone expresses Biblically-hostile, anti-Semitic, anti-Christian, anti-American, or anti-Israel beliefs, they are applauded and celebrated in the media for exercising their controversial Freedom of Speech. This is such gross hypocrisy. One big example of this double standard is the lamestream media's response to NFL player Colin Kaepernick's "take a knee" movement.

When a devout Christian Quarterback, Tim Tebow, had taken a knee in prayer to our Lord during games, the mainstream media would go berserk. Yet, when a "Black Power" Quarterback takes a knee in protest during our country's National Anthem, the same lamestream media cannot praise him enough. MSNBC has said of Kaepernick, "When a NFL player kneels in protest, it's *unifying*." A few years ago, the same network said (regarding Tim Tebow),

"Kneeling in prayer is *polarizing*." So, liberals seem to think that bringing God onto a football field is a horrible thing; but they also think that bringing divisive politics into the game is something to be celebrated. Sorry, my liberal friends, I assure you that it's most certainly the other way around.

The folks at MSNBC, and most of the media, are chock-full of double standards. Besides their contradictory opinions on NFL kneeling, another one of their many double standards has to do with us devout Christians refusing to participate in gay marriages. The Bakers, calligraphers, florists, photographers, tailors, or other Faith-based business owners denying services for gay weddings have been demonized as bigots by the media. The PC police are obsessed with forcing believers, like Jack Phillips of Masterpiece Cakeshop in Colorado, to bake a cake for a gay wedding.

Imagine if the Black Lives Matter activists were pressured to make a cake for the Ku Klux Klan. Do you think the media would call them "bigots" or discriminatory for refusing service? I highly doubt it. What if Democrats were forced to make a pro-Trump cake, or to provide services for a Trump Rally? I am sure that the media would be siding with the anti-Trumpers. What if Jews were told they had to bake a cake for Nazis? Obviously, they should *never* be expected to comply. I rest my case. It seems as if only God-fearing Christians are forced to violate their conscience and deeply held beliefs today.

Sadly, even after the landslide Republican Party victory in the 2016 Election, Christians are still under attack across this nation. The messages we are being sent from most liberal Americans are loud and clear: "Christians are NOT welcome" and "Conform *OR ELSE*." Even powerful corporations use money and influence to force Christians into submission. Apple, AMC, CBS, Coca Cola, Disney, Facebook, Marriott, Marvel, MGM, NBC, NCAA, NFL, Paypal, Sony, Time Warner, Twitter, and Viacom (just to name a few) are all pushing the LGBT agenda. The past few years, these companies all launched boycotts against any states attempting to pass Religious Liberty Bills.

For those not aware, Religious Freedom Laws are passed to protect us Christians and Jews from having to violate our Faith for any reason. All of the Companies that I mentioned above are hypocrites. They say they're fighting the laws in order to prevent discrimination. Meanwhile, they are all guilty of discriminating against those who adhere to Almighty God's Word. They claim to defend freedom, while at the same time, trampling or threatening freedoms of those with whom they disagree. It is nothing short of a war on Christians, plain and simple.

HGTV dropped the Benham Brothers' reality show, before it had even aired, because of their Biblical beliefs. A few years later, their friends, Chip and Joanna Gaines of HGTV's *Fixer Upper*, were demonized in the media for merely *attending* a church that preaches what the Bible says about Gay Marriage. *Duck Dynasty* patriarch, Phil Robertson, whipped up a firestorm in the media for daring to publicly speak what God says about homosexuality. All of these famous believers had come under fire, not for their own cooked up belief system - but for believing what the Word of God says. Sadly, there are many Christians nationally who endure the same kind of pressure from the LGBT Mafia, and who lose their businesses for refusing to violate their Faith.

Christian-owned Timbercreek Bed and Breakfast, of Illinois, was forced to pay a gay couple $80,000 for refusing to host a gay union ceremony. Immediately after Illinois recognized same-sex civil unions in 2011, a gay couple, Todd and Mark Wathen, had inquired as to whether or not Timbercreek would be hosting civil unions. Owner Jim Walder replied, "No. We only do weddings." The men had threatened to sue Walder and he replied, "the Bible trumps Illinois law, United States law and Global law. Please read John 3:16." The couple complained to the Illinois Human Rights Commission and won their case against Timbercreek.

In the Washington Supreme Court, there is a case involving a Christian grandmother. 73-year-old Baronelle Stutzman, owner of Arlene's Flowers, has been accused of "discrimination" against a gay couple. She had come under fire for declining to make flower arrangements for their wedding. Stutzman had served the couple, Robert Ingersoll and Curt Freed, for years; but she declined to do arrangements for their wedding because it violated her beliefs.

The owners of Sweet Cakes By Melissa bakery, in Oregon, were ordered to pay a $135,000 fine after they refused to bake a wedding cake for a Gay Marriage ceremony. The Oregon Bureau of Labor and Industries Commissioner who heard their case, Brad Avakian, said the Christian owners needed to be "rehabilitated." *Rehabilitated*? So believing the Holy Bible is a disease now?!

You should all be familiar with the case of Kentucky County Clerk, Kim Davis, who had actually been thrown into *prison* for refusing to violate her beliefs. Thank God that her story garnered enough media coverage to spark a huge uproar in the Christian community, otherwise she'd most likely still be behind bars today. Simply for adhering to God's Word! The uncomfortable question that believers should be asking today is… how many Kim Davis' are out there as we speak? How many Christians, who've gotten no media attention, are sitting in jail cells right now for refusing to violate their Faith? It is a difficult thought to ponder.

There are so many of our brothers and sisters in the Faith that are being sued and punished by the U.S. judicial system for being *falsely* accused of discrimination. The LGBT community are *not* victims, as they are so often portrayed. Rather, they are the ones who are really discriminating. What if a Christian group tried to hold church services inside of a gay club or resort? Would they be winning a discrimination lawsuit for being denied entry? I'll bet not. How about if a believer walked into an LGBT-themed print shop and asked to have Leviticus 18:22 printed on t-shirts? Would the establishment be forced to make clothing that made them feel uncomfortable? Would they be forced to pay a fine? I think we all know, full well, the answer to these questions is a resounding NO.

If the shoe were on the other foot, Christians would not be winning lawsuits for being discriminated against; and the number one reason for that is because we wouldn't be suing anyone who refuses us service. We just take our business elsewhere. We never set out to intentionally ruin another person's life, or to break them financially, simply because they hold different beliefs than we do. We do our best to influence and inspire others to believe the Word of God, but we don't *force* it on anyone (like we're always falsely accused of doing). Contrarily, as my friends the Benham Brothers point out, LGBT bullies force us to "accept" their lifestyle - then they force us to "celebrate" it - and now they are forcing us to "participate" in it.

If anybody in this country is forcing anything on anyone, it's the LGBT crowd forcing an agenda down everyone else's throat - not the other way around. Every single freedom-loving American, Christian or not, needs to stand united against this evil agenda of bullying others you disagree with into submission. Even Christian children, teens, and college students, aren't safe. School teachers, promoting the LGBT agenda, felt emboldened during the Obama years to discriminate against Christian students who dared object to our society's "new normal."

In 2017, a lesbian teacher in Florida actually forced students in her class to remove their Cross necklaces. One of the students reported that Lora Jane Reidas, her Math teacher, had approached her and said, "I need you to take your necklace off." When the student asked why, Riedas refused to explain and simply said, "It is disrespectful, and you have to take it off." The student says that she did not want to be disrespectful, "so I took it off, but I felt bad because I felt like I was being forced to deny my Faith." Riedas is a Gay-Straight Alliance sponsor, and engages in political activism in her classroom, which is decorated with LGBT propaganda. She has buttons displayed on her desk, facing students, stating "I Love My LGBT Students" and "*Proud* Public Employee."

Think about the left-wing outrage if a Christian teacher ever dared have John 3:16, "Pro-Life," or "I Love My Bible-believing Students" buttons displayed in their classroom. They'd be fired on day one. Yet, Riedas' superiors at the school have seemingly had no problem with her LGBT propaganda on full display. As if all this was not enough to get a God-fearing parent's blood boiling, the teacher also placed LGBT rainbow stickers on her students' folders without their consent. One of the Christian students who removed an LGBT sticker said that "Ms. Riedas' behavior toward me changed for the worse."

When Obama was in power, the Godless teachers across this nation cracked down on students who dared bring Bibles into the classroom. Like Riedas, they'd confiscated Crucifixes and banned God-related clothing. In one instance, a 2nd-grader in Texas had her Bible taken away during "read to myself time." Students were told to bring in personal books from home to read, but apparently the *Good Book* was off-limits. While anything having to do with the Faiths of Christianity and Judaism was being abolished from the schools during Obama's tenure, Islam was being force-fed to your kids. In mandated Common Core textbooks, our Faiths were not taught. When they were mentioned, they were mocked or put down. Yet, an entire chapter (of 30+ pages) was devoted to Islam!

Most major colleges in this country today are infested with far-left atheist professors who don't just question God, but they openly attack Him, mock the Holy Bible, and alienate or publicly disgrace any students who would dare disagree. Go to any secular campus today and tell a professor that you believe in God as our Creator, that Jesus Christ was born of a virgin, that He rose from the dead, and that the Holy Bible is the unerring Word of God. If you are really feeling bold, tell them you believe Jesus is *coming back*. The ignorant Godless "teachers" will shout you down and will laugh you to scorn. If you have never seen the Christian film *God's NOT Dead*, I recommend you do. It's a perfect portrayal of what life is like for believers on college campuses today.

Harvard College, like a majority of this nation's prestigious institutes of learning, had been originally established in 1636 as a Christian University to train clergy. Sadly, they are anything *but* Christian today. In March of 2018, it was reported that Harvard placed the university's largest Christian group on administrative probation for adhering to their Biblical beliefs. Harvard College Faith and Action was disciplined by the Office of Student Life because they "pressured a female member to resign for dating a woman." So, to be clear, a *Christian* group, whose members all believe the *Christian* Bible, asked a member living in unrepentant sin to resign. There is absolutely nothing wrong with this picture. Harvard's powers that be are slapping their God-fearing founders in the face by *punishing* the Faith they used to *preach*.

I like how Andrew T. Walker of *Weekly Standard* described the complete 180 which Harvard has taken from its inception. He wrote, "The shift at the University is so radical that while a few decades ago it took courage to be openly gay at Harvard, these days it takes a great deal of courage to be openly CHRISTIAN." Talk about hitting the nail on the head. Unfortunately, Harvard is not the only college persecuting Christians for their deeply held beliefs. Universities of Vanderbilt, Cal State, Bowdoin, Iowa, and Wayne State have been targeting Christian groups for probation, suspension, and even expulsion.

Vanderbilt's "Tolerance Policy" forced most Christian groups from off of its campus altogether. This is such a disgrace to the fabric of our country, as our very *first* schoolbook was the Bible. How far we have fallen as a Judeo-Christian Nation! Believe it or not, anti-God liberals became so emboldened under eight years of Obama, they are now attempting to *ban the Bible*. No joke. A bill in California, that is expected to pass in the Democrat-controlled

State Senate later this year (2018), aims to ban Faith-based books which "address issues of homosexuality or gender identity."

Assembly Bill 2943 declares Christian books or conferences, dealing with Biblical views on homosexuality or transgenderism, as "fraudulent" under the State's consumer fraud statute. The Bill becoming Law would *criminalize* and penalize all those who dare to share a "Biblical view on marriage." We have been living in an America that's been entrenched in extreme secularism for the past decade. Now, it appears our country has descended into flat out *paganism*. God help us. Even Christians in neighboring Canada are facing extreme pressure from their liberal leadership, led by Prime Minister Justin Trudeau.

In 2017, a Canadian Christian school had been ordered by a Public School Board to "cease reading or studying any Scripture" that was considered as "offensive" to certain individuals. Targeted Biblical verses included all those speaking against homosexuality, fornication, adultery, idolatry, and witchcraft. Battle River School Division, in Alberta, directed Cornerstone Christian Academy to refrain from teaching on Scripture that the board had determined "violates Alberta's human rights legislation." The school's vision statement says, "students will have a good working knowledge of the Bible as a foundation to their education." Unfortunately, their liberal School Board is dead set on changing that.

There have been many more disturbing developments coming out of Canada, and you can read about all of them on my website (*BiblicalSigns.com*). Their Prime Minister, Justin Trudeau, called Evangelical Christians "the *worst* part of Canadian society," and he was one of the very first world leaders to ever take part in a Gay Pride march. America was hell for Christians under Obama, and it's safe to say that our brothers and sisters to the North feel the exact same under Trudeau. We need to pray for Godly leaders to be raised up, not only here in our country - but in Canada, and in every other nation of this world!

While Christians in the West have faced extreme pressure for simply believing what the LORD has to say about things, we have not yet experienced the deadly persecution that our brothers and sisters across the globe have been enduring. Lord willing, we will not anytime soon! Satan has influenced so many around the world to persecute believers, but there is no question that his top recruits have been Islamic terrorists. The next chapter delves deep into the Latter-Day sign of terrorism.

JESUS SAID, BLESSED ARE THEY WHICH ARE PERSECUTED FOR RIGHTEOUSNESS' SAKE: FOR THEIRS IS THE KINGDOM OF HEAVEN. BLESSED ARE YE, WHEN MEN SHALL REVILE YOU, AND PERSECUTE YOU, AND SHALL SAY ALL MANNER OF EVIL AGAINST YOU FALSELY, FOR MY SAKE. REJOICE, AND BE EXCEEDING GLAD: FOR GREAT IS YOUR REWARD IN HEAVEN.

- MATTHEW 5:10-12

CHAPTER THREE

TERRORISM

JESUS SAID, AS THE DAYS OF NOAH WERE, SO SHALL ALSO THE
COMING OF THE SON OF MAN BE.

(IN THE DAYS OF NOAH) THE EARTH WAS FILLED WITH
VIOLENCE (TERRORISM).

- MATTHEW 24:37 & GENESIS 6:11

RECENTLY RELEASED FIGURES FROM the GPI (Global Peace
Index) revealed that worldwide terrorism has reached an *all-time
high*. According to the Peace Index, the annual number of terror
incidents has nearly *tripled* since 2011. That is only seven years
from the publication of this book. Also, the breadth of terrorism is
spreading; as there are now only 10 countries - out of nearly 250 -
that have not been victims of terror in recent years. Deaths from
terrorism have risen almost 1000% in the past decade in at least
35 countries. Deaths from terrorism in Europe, and specifically in
Belgium, Britain, and France, more than *doubled* since 2012. And
according to researchers at the Institute for Economics and Peace,
deaths from conflicts in Islamic countries are at a 25-year high.

The majority of the terrorist activity has been concentrated in
Mideast Muslim nations, to no surprise. Globally, there have been
around 30,000 Islamic terror attacks since the 9/11/2001 tragedy;
and well over 10,000 attacks "in the name of Allah," the god of

Islam, in just the past 5 years. That's over 2,000 every year! Since its inception, over 270-million human beings have been murdered by followers of that "peaceful religion" known as Islam. While liberal talking heads love saying, "not all Muslims are terrorists" or "ISIS perverts the religion," facts disagree. Islamic terrorists follow Muhammad's commands in the Quran more faithfully than the majority of Muslims in the world.

The moderate or Westernized Muslims attempt to spiritualize the literal commands of Allah to justify his many calls for "jihad" against infidels. Though, scholars all agree that when Muhammad wrote about jihad, it was never meant to be spiritualized. He had specifically meant to declare physical war on non-Muslims if they refuse to convert to Islam. I'll share some Quranic verses later in this chapter to prove, beyond a shadow of a doubt, that beheading infidels - cutting off their fingers and toes - burning them alive - throwing them off of highrise buildings - burying them up to their heads in sand - and crucifying them - can *never* be "spiritualized." Muhammad meant his words to be taken quite *literally*.

Historically, Muhammad was no "prophet." He was a military leader. He had laid siege to towns, massacring the men, raping the women and enslaving the children. He inspired his followers to battle when they did not feel that it was right to fight, promising them slaves and spoils if they did. He threatened them with hell if they did not. How different from our Holy Lord Jesus Christ and the *real* holy prophets of our true God, YHWH.

Today, most Muslims in America and the Western world are not living like their prophet. That is a good thing! Islamic terror groups, like the Islamic State (ISIS), are Muslims truly modeling their lives after Muhammad. Contrary to the widely held belief, which the lamestream liberal media promotes here in the West, this isn't a small movement of extremists in the religion of Islam. It's a large and growing movement. There are hundreds of Islamic terror groups globally, and it is estimated that 25% of the Muslim population are radicals. This means there are about 300-million Muslims in the world supporting or engaging in terror activities.

There have been more Christians and Jews brutally murdered by Islamists in the 20th century than in all previous 19 centuries *combined*, and roughly 100,000 Christians are murdered for their Faith *every year* by Muslim terrorists.

While prophesying to His disciples the many signs that would precede His return to Earth, Lord Jesus said that the world would be "as it was in the days of Noah." The Book of Genesis, Chapter 6 and verse 5, describes the human condition on Earth in Noah's days. The LORD said that "the wickedness of man was great in the earth, and that every imagination of the thoughts of his heart was only evil continually." He went on to say that all men were corrupt, with the exception of only Noah. In verse 11, we read, "the earth was filled with violence." In the Hebrew translation, the word used for violence can mean "terror."

It is important to note that God's attention is always centered on the Nation of Israel in the Bible. This is what makes Christ's Noah prophecy all the more exclusive to our day and age, because the Hebrew word used for "violence" in Genesis 6 is "HAMAS" - which means "shedding of innocent blood." For over 3-decades, Palestine's terrorist group has been called *Hamas*. It's interesting that the word used to describe terrorism, all the way back in the first Book of our Bible, is a name for one of Israel's greatest foes!

While Hamas, without a doubt, has committed the most terror attacks against Israelis in modern times, there've been many other groups that have attacked the Jewish State since its 1948 rebirth. Terror groups such as Hezbollah, the PLO (Palestine Liberation Organization), Islamic Jihad, Fatah, the Muslim Brotherhood, and ISIS, have all sought the destruction of Israel; but Hamas has, by far, been the most constant threat - hands down.

The Holy Bible interprets the Bible, and God planted a word that would only be truly relevant in this generation back in the very first Book of the Holy Scriptures. Jesus knew that the word "Hamas" was there, as He had penned Genesis with the Father through the Holy Spirit. In Matthew, Chapter 24 and verse 37, He was prophesying that the land in and around Israel would be filled with the terror of *Hamas*. For thousands upon thousands of years, there was no group of people called by that name. That is... until *our generation*. Since Israel's rebirth, there've been around 1,400 terror attacks - leaving about 3,500 dead and injuring over 14,000 innocent Israelis. Hamas, Hezbollah, and Islamic Jihad are all the proxies of Israel's biggest enemy on the world stage: *Iran*.

These terror groups all receive their weapon arsenals directly from Iran. The Islamic regime in Tehran is the largest funder and organizer of terrorism globally. If we ever want to truly win the "War on Terror," and destroy the deadly serpent threatening our world, then we must cut off the serpent's head - which is IRAN. The Iranians station the groups that I have mentioned strategically on the borders of Israel. These terrorists receive their marching orders directly from the Ayatollahs, and serve as hired hands of the anti-Israel regime. The close proximity of these groups to the Jewish State allows Iran to make war on Israel, without having the two nations ever engaged in direct conflict. Iran knows, full well, that they would lose a one-on-one war with Israel.

Sharing a mutual hatred of the Jewish people, the Palestinians - led by Hamas - are more than happy to do Iran's dirty work. They use whatever weapons they can get their hands on to inflict terror upon Israel. In recent years, their weapons of choice have been guns, knives, machetes, molotov cocktails, axes, grenades, flaming kites, vehicles, and rockets. Around 20,000 rockets have been launched into Israel from the Hamas-controlled Gaza Strip since 2001. Over 5,000 of those have been fired upon Israel in the past 4 years alone. Here in America, ignorant liberals scream for "gun control" to prevent mass-casualty terror attacks. What they fail to understand is that mass murderers weaponize just about anything, as Palestinians prove.

Biblically-illiterate politicians do not recognize that we are in a spiritual battle between good and evil, and that guns are simply one of many tools which a terrorist will use to take innocent lives. Banning guns will *never stop* the plague of terrorism. Along with the many weapons that I have already mentioned, which the terror groups threatening Israel use on a daily basis, Islamists have also used planes and pressure cookers. Why aren't Democrats pushing for a "pressure cooker ban" here in America? Such a bomb can leave dozens dead. The truth is that it is not guns, knives, bombs, vehicles, or even pressure cookers that are murdering thousands of innocent people globally. It is the dangerous ideology of Islam. It's the head, heart, and hands behind the weapon that is to blame.

Unfortunately, there are many who cannot comprehend this reality. Liberals blame anything, and anyone, except the terrorists themselves. When Israelis are murdered by Palestinian terrorists, Israel is portrayed as the "bad guy" when they retaliate. When us Christians are murdered by Islamists, *we*'re blamed for provoking them with *Islamophobia*. When Americans are murdered, assault weapons are to blame. When an Islamic husband and wife shoot up an office Christmas Party, "poor vetting" of immigrants is to blame. When an Islamic shooter goes postal at a U.S. Army base, "workplace violence" or mental health are to blame. It seems as if every terror attack carried out by a Muslim, especially in the U.S., gets labeled any and every thing other than what it is - *Islamic*.

The civilized world will never defeat the scourge of Islamic terrorism until we can learn to call it what it is. We need to call a spade a spade. I really love how Israeli Prime Minister, Benjamin Netanyahu, puts it - "If it looks like a duck, walks like a duck, and quacks like a duck, then what is it? That's right, *it's a duck*... It's time the world started calling a duck *a duck*." Can I get an amen?! Politically correct thinking to appease radical Muslims does not work. It never will. So long as the Quran is read by billions across the globe (the book that contains 100+ verses calling for Muslims to "strike terror" in the hearts of unbelievers), they'll always hate us. They'll always want to murder us. You can't get around it. It is just the way it is.

Until the world realizes that Islamic terror is not spawned by radical clerics and mosques, nor by propaganda, or campaigns in the Middle East, but solely by the "holy" book of Islam, terrorism isn't going anywhere. For not one of the most dangerous terror groups in the world today are Christian, Jewish, Buddhist, Sikh, Hindu, or any other religion for that matter. They are *all* Islamic. Islam is a cancer spreading across the globe. It infects, and then systematically destroys, every society that it touches. On average, every 12th verse of the Quran speaks of Allah's hatred for the infidels. It calls for our death, forced conversion, or subjugation. Here are some examples -

QURAN 2:191-193: "KILL them wherever you find them... Fight them until there is no more Fitnah (disbelief) and worship is for Allah alone."

QURAN 3:151: "Soon shall we cast TERROR into the hearts of the unbelievers."

QURAN 5:33: "They should be murdered or CRUCIFIED or their hands and their feet should be cut off on opposite sides or they should be imprisoned."

QURAN 8:12: "I will cast TERROR into the hearts of those who disbelieve. Therefore strike off their heads and strike off every fingertip of them."

QURAN 8:39: "FIGHT with them until there is no more fitna (disbelief in Allah) and religion is all for Allah."

QURAN 9:5: "SLAY the idolaters wherever you find them, and take them captive and besiege them and lie in wait for them in every ambush."

QURAN 9:29: "FIGHT those who believe not in Allah."

QURAN 9:30: "And the JEWS say: Ezra is the son of Allah; and the CHRISTIANS say: The Messiah is the son of Allah; these are the words of their mouths; they imitate the saying of those who disbelieved before; may Allah DESTROY them."

QURAN 47:3-4: "When you meet those who disbelieve smite at their necks (behead) till when you have KILLED and wounded many of them."

BUKHARI 52:177: "Allah's apostle said, The Hour will not be established until you fight with the JEWS, and the stone behind which a Jew will be hiding will say. 'O Muslim! There is a Jew hiding behind me, so KILL HIM.'"

BUKHARI 52:220: "Allah's apostle said... I have been made victorious with TERROR."

MUSLIM 1:33: "I've been commanded to FIGHT against people till they testify that there is no god but Allah, that Muhammad is the messenger of Allah."

MUSLIM 19:4294: "Fight in the name of Allah and in his way. Fight against those who disbelieve in Allah. Make a HOLY WAR."

MUSLIM 20:4645: "JIHAD in the way of Allah!"

TABARI 7:97: "The Prophet (Muhammad) declared, 'KILL ANY JEW who falls under your power.'"

TABARI 9:69: "KILLING unbelievers is a small thing to us."

Though politically incorrect when us Christians or Jews point it out, the Quran admits Muslims do not worship the same God as Judaism and Christianity (Quran 109:1-6). Salvation is *achieved* in Islam by means of martyrdom and by murdering infidels (Jews & Christians). The God and Father of the Jews and Christians, YHWH, teaches that Salvation is *received* by faith in the sacrifice of His only begotten Son, Jesus Christ - who was crucified on our behalf. Islam's god wants you to die *for him*, while our God died *for us*. What a difference! Our Holy Book's LORD commands us to "do no murder"; while, as I've just proved through the Quran itself, Allah is *all for* fighting - slaying - killing - beheading - and committing acts of terror "in his name."

Islam is the polar opposite of Christianity and Judaism; and the main reason Muslims hate us Christians and Jews so much is because their god is *Satan*. Lucifer fell from his place in Heaven because he wanted to BE God (Isaiah 14:13-14) and now, through Islam, he finally can achieve his age-old goal to be worshipped *as God*. Jesus said the devil "was a murderer from the beginning" (John 8:44), and there's no other group on Planet Earth with more murderers in its ranks than Islam. And besides Satan, there is also another archenemy of YAHWEH mentioned throughout the pages of our Holy Bible - and that's the chief of the false gods, *Baal*.

What didn't surprise me, in my studies, is that the name Allah is derived from the name of Baal. According to the Encyclopedia of Religion, Arabs knew of Baal as Allah long before Muhammad had ever propped him up to be worshipped as the supreme god of

Muslims. Before the author of Islam came around, the Arabs had recognized many false gods and goddesses. Each Arab tribe had their own deities, and 360 gods were worshipped in their lands. There was a god for every day of their calendar year. Baal/Allah was the name that was assigned to each tribe's particular "high god." Baal/Allah was known as the "warrior god," and also as the "moon god." The crescent moon was the symbol for Baal, and it is today the widely recognized symbol for the religion of Islam.

Baal was YHWH's chief enemy all throughout the pages of the Old Testament, and Satan is the adversary of God in the New Testament. So, could Lucifer be Baal and vice versa? Biblically, it makes all the sense in the world. It is also important to note that Allah is referred to as "the great *deceiver*" (Quran 3:54 & 8:30). That title should ring a bell in the minds of believers, as someone is referred to as the great deceiver in our Book - and that someone is Satan. So, if Baal is Satan and Allah is Baal, then it is hard for anyone to deny that ALLAH IS SATAN.

The Book of Revelation tells us that the devil will make war on believers, and that we will be slain and *beheaded*. What group of people on Earth do we see beheading Christians today? From medieval times up until a few years ago, the answer was *no one*. Yet, *in our day*, there is a clear cut *someone* - and that would be Islamists. There can be no denying that Islamic terrorism, and the religion of Islam itself, is so truly *of the devil*.

AND I SAW THE SOULS OF THEM THAT WERE BEHEADED FOR THE WITNESS OF JESUS, AND FOR THE WORD OF GOD.

- REVELATION 20:4

CHAPTER FOUR

THE FIG TREE

JESUS SAID, NOW LEARN A PARABLE OF THE FIG TREE; WHEN
HIS BRANCH IS YET TENDER, AND PUTTETH FORTH LEAVES,
YE KNOW THAT SUMMER IS NIGH.

- MATTHEW 24:32

THE GOSPEL OF MATTHEW, Chapter 24, is arguably the Holy
Bible's most comprehensive account of the "Last Days" signs that
herald Christ's return - and were given to us by Jesus Himself. In
verse 34, He told His disciples that "the generation" witnessing
the fulfillment of His signs would be alive in the season of His
Second Coming. In verses 32-34, He mentioned the blossoming
of the "*fig tree*" - and that is the most important sign of them all.
Without this integral sign being fulfilled, all the rest of His signs
could be taking place at once and mean *nothing* prophetically.

The reason being that Jews and Christians have experienced
persecution for thousands of years, Earth has experienced a lot of
powerful earthquakes, false prophets have been around since the
earliest days of Christianity, extreme weather has occurred since
the days of Noah, and there've been wars in every generation. But
for around 2,000 years, since Jesus ascended into Heaven, there
was no Nation of Israel on Planet Earth. The "fig tree" that Jesus
was referring to was, no doubt, ISRAEL.

Our Lord said that when we witness all of the signs He listed in Matthew 24 taking place, during the generation of the Jewish State's rebirth, we'd *"know"* that His return is *"near."* Throughout history, there have been a lot of Christians who believed that they were *the* generation who'd live to see Him coming in the clouds; but that was impossible with no Israel on the map. I'm glad those generations lived with the hope of seeing Christ come back; but the fact remains that if they lived any time before 1948, there was no way they could be the generation that Jesus had spoken of.

After the Jews had been exiled from their Promised Land by the Assyrians, Babylonians, Romans, Muslims, Turks, and others, they were scattered across the globe. Thoughts of their Biblical Homeland ever being resurrected appeared dismal, and virtually impossible. They had one sure and strong hope to cling to though: God's Eternal Word. In the Bible, the LORD had never broken even one promise that He'd ever made to Israel. He had promised in His Word, numerous times, to return the Jewish people to their God-given Land in the Last Days and to reestablish their Nation. The reestablishment of the Jewish State was Jesus' sign of the fig tree blossoming *fulfilled.*

When our Lord eventually makes His imminent return, every believer should know that He comes back down to defend and to save Israel from certain destruction in the Battle of Armageddon. Christ will personally fight and defeat Antichrist, as well as all of the nations who join him in making war on God's chosen Nation. Jesus will then rule and reign from Israel's Capital of Jerusalem, as King of kings and Lord of lords, over the whole world. Until there was actually a Nation of Israel on the earth, none of these prophecies could be fulfilled. For over 2,500 years, there was no "Israel." In May of 1948, that changed.

Before I go further, I'm sure many of you may be asking how I can be so sure that the fig tree which Jesus referred to was truly the Nation of Israel? When in doubt, examine the entirety of the

Scriptures to figure it out. When God mentioned the "fig tree" in Jeremiah 24:5, Hosea 9:10, and Joel 1:6-7, He referred to Israel in every instance. There is no one who can argue otherwise. So, that settles that. Now, back to 1948... 70 years ago, on May 14th, the ancient Biblical Nation of Israel was officially reborn. The LORD prophesied, about 3,000 years ago, that the Jews would be exiled from their Holy Land for just over 2,500 Years. After that period of separation, He said He'd return them to their Promised Land. We read in Ezekiel 37:21...

"THUS SAITH THE LORD GOD; BEHOLD, I WILL TAKE THE CHILDREN OF ISRAEL FROM AMONG THE HEATHEN, WHITHER THEY BE GONE, AND WILL GATHER THEM ON EVERY SIDE, AND BRING THEM INTO THEIR OWN LAND."

In 606 BC, the Jewish exile began. In the exact number of Biblically-prophesied years later, God would fulfill His age-old promise to the Jewish people. He gathered them from all nations of the world, wherever they had been scattered, and brought them *back* into their ancient God-given Land. I love the mathematical prophecy found in the Book of Ezekiel. In Chapter 4, verses 4-6, the LORD said to the prophet...

"LIE THOU ALSO UPON THY LEFT SIDE, AND LAY THE INIQUITY OF THE HOUSE OF ISRAEL UPON IT: ACCORDING TO THE NUMBER OF THE DAYS THAT THOU SHALT LIE UPON IT THOU SHALT BEAR THEIR INIQUITY. FOR I HAVE LAID UPON THEE THE YEARS OF THEIR INIQUITY, ACCORDING TO THE NUMBER OF THE DAYS, THREE HUNDRED AND NINETY DAYS: SO SHALT THOU BEAR THE INIQUITY OF THE HOUSE OF ISRAEL. AND WHEN THOU HAST ACCOMPLISHED THEM, LIE AGAIN ON THY RIGHT SIDE, AND THOU SHALT BEAR THE INIQUITY OF THE HOUSE OF JUDAH FORTY DAYS: I HAVE APPOINTED THEE EACH DAY FOR A YEAR."

God was speaking of judgment upon Israel, as a whole, but mentioned Judah separately from Israel because (at that time) the Nation was split up into two Kingdoms. Judah represented the Southern Kingdom. There were to be 390 days of judgment upon Israel's ten Northern Tribes, and 40 days upon the two Southern Tribes - which equaled 430 years of judgment against the Jewish State in total. Israel was taken into captivity by the Babylonians for 70 years. So, 430 minus 70 years fulfilled during the captivity = 360 years remaining in the judgment. There are many who have wondered where the remaining 360-year judgment was fulfilled in Israel's history following the Babylonian captivity. We must look to the "7X factor" of God's judgment for the answer.

Biblical scholars cannot find a specific captivity or dispersion to fulfill the 360 years left in the judgment, but a closer look into Leviticus reveals God's seven-times warning (Leviticus 26:18, 21, 27-28 and 33). In the verses, the LORD warned Israel that if they continued in disobedience then He would multiply their judgment by "seven." God always says what He means, and means what He says. So, applying the 7X factor to the 360 years of judgment yet to be carried out against them, 2,520 years of judgment remain.

YHWH gave the Jews the most sophisticated calendar on the earth. It's both a Lunar and Solar calendar. The Hebrew calendar uses a 360-day Lunar (and Prophetic) year, and adds a leap month on specific years to coincide with the Solar cycle. The Bible uses 360-day years for prophecies, and it expects us to add appropriate leap months on schedule. The easiest way we can unravel this prophecy is to first convert it into days - 2,520 years x 360 days = 907,200 days of judgment remaining after Babylonian captivity. We then convert 907,200 days into 365.25 day Solar (Gregorian) years (the .25 adjusts for leap years), and 2,483.78 years remain.

Starting with the 70 years of Babylonian captivity, we arrive at 536 BC. We then add 2,483 years of judgment which are left, plus one year (because there is no 0 BC or AD), and we arrive at

1948 AD! How amazing is that?! The LORD's truly *right on time* all of the time. In the spring of 1948, Israel was officially declared and globally recognized as a nation again for the first time in over 2,500 years. HalleluYah. But wait, there's more! The time period of the Jewish people being exiled from the Holy Land by Babylon to the year the Babylonians destroyed Jerusalem was **19 years**; and the time period of Israel regaining their Homeland in 1948 to reclaiming Jerusalem as their Capital City in 1967 was **19 years**!

God had mirrored the years of exile and return for a sure sign that it was His Divine Hand at work. It was in June of 1967, when Islamic armies surrounding Israel attacked the Jewish State from every border. They were looking to finish what Hitler started by attempting to wipe out the Jewish people and the Nation of Israel from the face of the earth. A small number of Israeli forces were greatly outnumbered by tens of thousands of troops; but the Jews not only defended their Nation valiantly, after only a Six-Day War they recaptured their ancient Capital of Jerusalem. Islamists had controlled the Holy City ever since taking it from the Christians centuries earlier. Israel defeated about a half-dozen hostile nations in less than *one week*.

It is crystal clear, to all who study the War, that the LORD was with His beloved Nation of Israel. Historians call the Israeli military victory "nothing short of a miracle." The Six-Day War had also mirrored an ancient battle in the Holy Bible to a tee. In Joshua, Chapter 6, verses 3-4, we find that the Israelite Army won the victory at Jericho in only six days -

"COMPASS THE CITY, ALL YE MEN OF WAR, AND GO ROUND ABOUT THE CITY ONCE. THUS SHALT THOU DO SIX DAYS."

By the 7th day, Joshua and his army had obtained the victory - just as the Israeli Army did in 1967. There can be no doubt that the LORD, Himself, fought on behalf of Israel on both occasions. He always has, and He always will.

Now, do you remember when I said Jesus told His disciples that "the generation" which witnessed the rebirth of Israel would also be the one living during the season of His return? Well, the Bible tells us that a generation ranges from 70-80 years (Psalms 90:10). In 2018, Israel celebrated the 70th Anniversary of rebirth. 70 years! Biblically, that puts us right at the end of a generation. The number 70 is also very important in Israel's history.

70 Israelites went down into Egypt (Exodus 1:5), Moses had appointed 70 elders of Israel (Numbers 11:16), and Daniel spoke of the prophetical 70 weeks (Daniel 9:24). Lord Jesus sent out 70 disciples to preach the Gospel in Luke 10, the Israelites spent 70 years in Babylonian captivity, it was 70 years from the time that Christ was born to the time of the destruction of Jerusalem's Holy Temple, and on the 70th Anniversary of the Jewish State's rebirth the U.S. Embassy opened in Israel's eternal Capital of Jerusalem.

I truly believe the Lord is at the gates, and ready to make His descent back to Earth. The Rapture could occur any day now, or at any hour, because the "Last Days" prophecies which have yet to be fulfilled are Tribulation prophecies. We believers will not be here for the seven-year period of Hell on Earth. Jesus promised that we would "escape" that hour of judgment which would come upon the whole world (Luke 21:36). He was clear that He would keep us "out of" it (Revelation 3:10).

I can give many reasons why the historic 70th Anniversary of Israel's rebirth could lead to something Biblically monumental on the horizon. For starters, the Hebrew year preceding the 70th year was 5777. The number 777 is attributed to our Father in Heaven, YHWH, for many reasons. It is also attributed to His Father-Son relationship with our Lord Jesus Christ, Israel's Messiah. Written in Hebrew, "YHWH in Yeshua Messiah" gives the number 777. If that, in itself, is not awesome enough, "Yeshua saves" in Hebrew also gives 777. The Holy Name YAHWEH appears as 777 when written in the Hebrew as well. If there were such a thing as the best number in the world, 777 would unquestionably be it!

In the Hebrew Year 5777 (which took place on our Western calendar between 2016-17), we celebrated the 50th Anniversary of the reunification of Israel's Holy Capital Jerusalem. Also, 5777 closed out the Biblical "Jubilee Year" (only coming around once every fifty years). It followed the "Shemitah Year" (coming once every seven years), and it was the year an accurate 800-year-old Rabbinical prophecy stated would "begin the season of Messiah's Coming" (in our case - His *return*).

Rabbi Judah Ben Samuel was a respected Talmudic scholar in Germany. Just before he had died, in the year 1217, he prophesied that Ottoman Turks would rule over Jerusalem for eight Jubilees. 8 x 50 = 400 years. Turks had indeed taken control of Jerusalem 300 years after his death, in 1517 - and his prophecy came to pass when they lost the Holy City in 1917 - 400 years later! Amazing. The Rabbi went on to prophesy that, after eight Jubilees, the 9th Jubilee would have Jerusalem being "a no-man's-land." The 9th Jubilee was from 1917 to 1967. He was *right on* again with his prophecy. The City was placed under British Mandate in 1917 by the League of Nations, and it literally belonged to NO nation.

Rabbi Samuel then stated that, in the 10th Jubilee, "Jerusalem would be controlled by Israel" - and the City *has been* ever since the Six-Day War of 1967! His prophecy concluded with "*then* the Messianic End Times would begin." The "then" refers to the end of 10th Jubilee and beginning of the new, which would be 2017! If this Rabbi was 100% accurate about everything else, we should take his Messiah prophecy very seriously.

I expect 2018 to be significant for Israel, prophetically, due to a fascinating 7-8-7 pattern. Biblically-relevant things concerning Israel, over the past century, have occurred in a year ending with a 7 - followed by a year ending with an 8 - and followed by a year ending with a 7. So, a year ending in an 8 would most likely be the year of the next big event concerning Israel.

In **1917**, the 400-year rule of the Ottomans over the Land of Israel ended; and British Prime Minister Balfour penned a historic declaration for a Jewish Homeland in Israel. In **1948**, the Nation was reborn. In **1967**, Israel miraculously won the Six-Day War and had reunified Jerusalem. With 2018 ending in an 8, could the thought-provoking 7-8-7 pattern continue? It already may have. After U.S. Presidents promising to do so for nearly 25 years, but never following through, President Donald Trump finally moved America's Embassy to Israel's eternal Capital in 2018. That was, as he would describe it, HUGE.

There is one last thing that bears mentioning. On November 14th, 2016, just after the kickoff of the year 5777, the Moon made its closest approach to Planet Earth in nearly 70 years. It will not be that close again until the year 2034. The 5777 Supermoon was extremely rare, and was the largest in our century. I mention the celestial event because of the significance of the last time that the Moon and Earth had been in such close proximity. The year just so happened to be 1948, which was the year that the fig tree had re-blossomed! Are you looking up yet?!

The Word of God teaches that "He appointed the Moon for seasons" (Psalms 104:19). A "season" in the Bible doesn't always mean spring, summer, fall, or winter. A season could also be His appointed time for grace, mercy, sowing, reaping, wrath, war, or prophetic fulfillment. Given all of the recent signs in the Moon, including the Blood Moon Tetrad of the recent Shemitah Year, I suspect we are living in a season of something truly historic. Any believer who can ignore the signs occurring all around us must be spiritually blind. God has been trying to alert us to something big coming on the horizon, and I truly believe that the "something" will be a *Someone*.

Will this generation, which is coming to a close, finally be the one that's raptured, endures the Tribulation, and witnesses Jesus' long-awaited return? I believe the answer is YES. Israel is finally back where they've always belonged, and the nations of the world are allying together to make war on the Jewish State - just as they are prophesied to. This means Israel's returning Messiah and their ultimate defender in the Armageddon battle is coming back down *soon*. One of the main reasons the nations come against Israel, in the end, is their obsession with the Jews' Capital of Jerusalem. That is what the coming chapter is about - the past, present, and future of the Holiest City on God's green earth.

FOR THE LORD WILL HAVE MERCY ON JACOB, AND WILL YET CHOOSE ISRAEL, AND SET THEM IN THEIR OWN LAND: AND THE STRANGERS SHALL BE JOINED WITH THEM, AND THEY SHALL CLEAVE TO THE HOUSE OF JACOB.

- ISAIAH 14:1

CHAPTER FIVE

JERUSALEM

THUS SAITH THE LORD OF HOSTS; I WILL BRING THEM, AND
THEY SHALL DWELL IN THE MIDST OF JERUSALEM: AND THEY
SHALL BE MY PEOPLE, AND I WILL BE THEIR GOD, IN TRUTH
AND IN RIGHTEOUSNESS.

- ZECHARIAH 8:8

DECEMBER 6TH, 2017, WAS a historic day for the United States of America and for God's chosen Nation of Israel. In what I call the greatest day of Donald Trump's Presidency, the POTUS gave a live address to the Nation and to the world officially recognizing Jerusalem as Israel's Capital. He also announced that he'd keep one of his most important Campaign promises, by directing the State Department to begin preparations for moving the Embassy from Tel Aviv to Jerusalem. The move was met by the rejoicing of Holy Bible-believing Christians and Jews, expressing thanks to the 45th President.

Of course, the anti-Semitic Muslims, liberals, atheists, and all Biblically-ignorant Americans, harshly criticized and condemned Trump. At the end of the day, the only opinion that ever matters is that of Almighty God. His Word makes crystal clear that Trump's actions, regarding Jerusalem, were undoubtedly pleasing to Him. I expected to see violent protests in Palestine, and in the Muslim world at large, following the President's announcement. They are always looking for an excuse to act like carnal animals. Islamists who hate Jews, Christians, Israel, and America - with a passion - rioted and burned our flags in Gaza, Turkey, Jordan, and across the Middle East. Hamas terrorists in Palestine threatened to "open the doors of hell," and a "third intifada," against the Jewish State.

Why the uproar over Trump's Jerusalem proclamation and his announcement to finally move our Embassy to Israel's Capital? Because the Muslims want our God's most Holy City, the most important piece of real estate to the Jews, to be the future Capital of Palestine. They were angry Trump publicly acknowledged the over 4,000-year-old Biblical truth that Jerusalem is the God-given property of Israel *alone*. It has *never* belonged to the Palestinians. It has never belonged to anyone else, in God's eyes, except Israel. Jerusalem may have been occupied by strangers, over the course of thousands of years, but it has *always* belonged to *His* people.

Historically, Jerusalem has always been, currently is, and will forever remain, the Capital of the Nation of Israel. No one who examines the history and facts surrounding Jerusalem could ever say, with a clear conscience, that the Palestinians have a claim to any piece of the Holy Land. There is not one shred of evidence on Earth to support that. No matter how many anti-Israel resolutions the Godless United Nations have passed or will pass, the LORD has made it abundantly clear that Jerusalem - and the entire Holy Land of Israel - was gifted to the Jewish people as an "everlasting possession." So, it does not matter what the Muslims say or what the world's leaders may think. No one can ever change the facts or unalterable truth about the Holy Land of God.

The UN, Islamic world, and the global media, refer to Israel's most treasured ancient cities as "illegal settlements" or the "West Bank" to deny Israel's claims to the Promised Land - which date back over 4-millennia. They refer to Israel as an "occupier" of land that they think belongs to the Palestinians, on the grounds of Israel reclaiming some of its Holiest Land in 1967's Six-Day War.

Since Jews were not "exterminated" from the Land in that War, as the allied Muslim nations hoped, the Palestinians who left (before the war) chose to remain in nearby Islamic nations. They refused to return to their homes, as long as Jews remained in the Land. Today's Palestinians falsely claim their ancestors were forced out, that Jews occupy their land, and that they have a "right to return."

The truth is that the Palestinians do not want to return to the Land and live alongside the Jews, just as the Muslims of 1948 and 1967 did not. They want what the terror group, Hamas, wants: to drive the Jews out of the Land and into the Mediterranean Sea. That is why every so-called Peace Plan between the Israelis and Palestinians has failed - because Muslims do not want peace with Israel. They want Israel *gone*. The only peaceful future Palestine desires is one where there is *no Israel*. They are going to be very disappointed in the end, because God says that will never happen. Israel abides "forever" (Joel 3:20).

There is not one inch of the Biblical Holy Land that belongs to Palestine. Not even one centimeter. Israelis aren't "occupying" anything, but rather they are exactly where the LORD has always determined them to dwell. The Land which God deeded to them is actually supposed to be 300,000 square miles. That is a far cry from the mere 8,600 square miles that makes up the modern-day Nation of Israel. The question that we should all be asking in the conflict between Israel and Palestine today is: if Israel currently possesses under 9,000 square miles of land, then who possesses the other 18.5-million acres of the Jews' Promised Land?

It is only in discovering the answer to this question that we come to the realization: there truly are "occupiers" in the Middle East today, and Israel is certainly *not* one of them! Yet, the world is always calling for tiny Israel to give up Land-for-peace - *never* their Muslim neighbors. This is primarily due to our generation's Biblical ignorance, lack of historical knowledge, or just unbridled anti-Semitism. As to who is occupying the other 291,000 square miles of Israel's God-given Land, we must examine the original borders of Israel - mapped out by the LORD in the Scripture.

The promise of the Land inheritance had first been made to Abraham in Genesis 15:18-21, renewed to his son Isaac, and then to Isaac's son Jacob (Israel) in Genesis 28:13. The Land had been described, in terms of the territory, in Exodus 23:31. Other verses in our Bible describing the Land allotment are found in Genesis 17:8, Numbers 34:1-15, Deuteronomy 1:7 - 11:24 - 19:8, Ezekiel 47:13-20, Judges 20:1, 1st Samuel 3:20, 2nd Samuel 3:10 - 17:11 - 24:2-15, 1st Kings 4:25, 1st Chronicles 21:2 and 2nd Chronicles 30:5. Some of these verses reveal that the modern-day nations of Palestine, Egypt, Iraq, Jordan, Lebanon, Saudi Arabia, Sudan, and Syria, are all occupying Israel's Land - *not the other way around.* I wish that this world would get educated in history!

The real conflict in the Middle East today should not be over the lie that Israel has "illegal settlements" on so-called Palestinian land, but should be about how the Palestinians (and *all* of Israel's neighbors) are illegally possessing Holy Land that God has given solely to the Jewish people. As I previously mentioned, the total area of Land making up the modern-day State of Israel is under 9,000 square miles. The size of the country is equivalent to the size of New Jersey. Meanwhile, many of the Islamic nations that I mentioned (who are always shouting at Israel to give up land to Palestinians for "peace") are *much* larger.

Saudi Arabia is nearly one-million square miles, Iran is over 600,000, Egypt is around 400,000, Turkey is over 300,000, Iraq is nearly 200,000, Syria is over 70,000, and Jordan is about 35,000 square miles. How come Palestine's fellow Muslim nations aren't offering up land for their so-called "refugee" brothers and sisters to dwell in for a future Palestinian State? They have far more land to spare than Israel. Think about it, if the Islamic countries loved Palestine (like they claim) as much as they hate Israel, Palestine could be a much bigger piece of real estate than Israel is today.

Egypt, Jordan, and Saudi Arabia all neighbor Palestine. These three nations have 1,440,000 square miles of land combined. You mean to tell me they can't each shave off a sliver of land to create a nation state for the Palestinians? They can't spare 5,000 square miles between the three of them? It'd solve the Israeli-Palestinian conflict *today*. At the end of the day, they really don't want peace between Jews and Arabs. They want war. They desire Israel to be destroyed. There is no denying what God wants, and that's for the Jews to remain right where they are.

The LORD promised that, once He returned the Jews to their ancient Land, they "would never again be removed" (Amos 9:15). He says that the Holy City, Jerusalem, and entirety of the Holy Land is the "property of Israel" nearly 1,000 times in the Bible. Allah, the god of Islam, mentions Jerusalem 0 times in the Quran. That's right... *ZERO*. Jerusalem is known as the "City of David," and the "City of the Great King (Jesus)." When Christ returns to Earth, His feet stand upon the Mount of Olives - which is located on Jerusalem's eastern border. He will then personally do away with the enemies of Israel. In the end, it will be Israel and God versus the entire world - *literally*.

Zechariah the prophet, in Chapter 12 of the book bearing his name, says, "all nations will come against Jerusalem" in the Last Days. That prophecy inches closer to fulfillment, as almost every nation on Earth opposed the President's Jerusalem announcement. In World War 3, which the Bible calls Armageddon, the LORD gathers all nations of the world to battle in the valley of Megiddo. It is in this final battle between the armies of God and armies of Satan that He'll judge the nations, and destroy anyone who came against Israel. Joel 3:2 warns the nations to not have a hand in dividing Israel's Land. Yet, in our day and age, that is the number one goal of the United Nations.

They have long been pushing, and now stronger than ever, for the division of Israel - specifically Jerusalem. All nations of this world, who are rebelling against the Word of God, will someday pay the price for their disobedience. God judges the nations of the world according to how they treat His beloved Nation of Israel. If they bless the Jewish State, they'll be blessed. If they curse Israel, they will be cursed (Genesis 12:3 and Numbers 24:9). The reason God gets so angry with nations for attempting to divide His Holy Land is because of just that: it's *His Land* - not United Nations' land, not Palestinian land, not Islamic land, not Christian land, not American land, not European land, and not even Jewish or Israeli land for that matter. It is the LORD's Property.

It's His to give, and His to take. It is the only God-given piece of real estate on the planet, and YHWH has deeded the Land as an "eternal" gift to just one nation: *Israel*. Even the Jewish State cannot place any land on the negotiating table in a future "peace" agreement with the Palestinians, because it is not theirs to deal - only God's. The basis for Palestinians claiming that they have any right to the Land is actions of an anti-Semitic Roman emperor of old, called Hadrian.

In 130 AD, after Jews had been expelled from their Promised Land by the Romans (about a century after Christ's death on the Cross), the Land was renamed "Palestine" by Hadrian. He chose the name because it represented an ancient enemy of the Jews, the Philistines. Hadrian paganized the Holy Land and desecrated the Holy City, Jerusalem. He decreed Roman maps would no longer use Biblical names of "Judea" or "Israel" for the Land. He erased the names in an attempt to scrub from history any Jewish claims to the Holy Land. Hence, due to Hadrian's hatred for the Jews, we have a society today deceived to believe the ancient Land belongs to Israel's enemies (Philistines-Palestinians) instead of its rightful owners, the Hebrews.

Jewish presence in the Holy Land, and specifically Jerusalem, is a presence far surpassing the rule of any other nation, people, race, or religion, since the dawn of time. You'd have to go back to

3500 BC to find the very first Jewish settlement in Jerusalem. If you're not good at math, that is over 5,500 years ago. Around the year 1865 BC, we read of Melchizedek - King of Jerusalem (then known as "Salem" - Genesis 14:18-20). Melchizedek is believed to have been the Lord Jesus Christ, coming down to commune with Abraham (Abram) - the forefather of Israel (Hebrews 7:1-3). In Joshua 18:28, we read that Jerusalem would be the inheritance of the Tribe of Benjamin - one of Israel's twelve sons.

In 1000 BC, King David claimed and declared Jerusalem as the Capital of Israel. In 960 BC, King Solomon (who was David's son) erected the first Jewish Temple in Jerusalem. In 721 BC, the Jews expanded the City. Biblically and Archaeologically, we have every proof that David, Solomon, and virtually all of the Kings of Israel, had ruled and reigned from Jerusalem (2nd Samuel, 1st & 2nd Kings, 1st & 2nd Chronicles). In 586 BC, when Jews were in captivity under the Babylonians, Jerusalem was all but destroyed. Between 539-516 BC, Cyrus the Great conquered the Babylonian Empire and had allowed Jews to live safely in Jerusalem. He also permitted the new Temple to be built.

Between 445-425 BC, Nehemiah the prophet rebuilt the walls of the Holy City. Between 332-141 BC, Alexander the Great had conquered Jerusalem and instituted Greek rule over Jews there. In 141 BC, the Hasmonean Dynasty began and Jews had once again expanded the City. In 63 BC, Roman General Pompey had taken Jerusalem and instituted Roman rule over Jews. In 37 BC, King Herod restructured the Temple and also added retaining walls. In the year 0 AD, our Lord Jesus Christ (Israel's Promised Messiah and King of the Jews) was born. Shortly thereafter, He was taken to Jerusalem to be presented to the LORD (YHWH). In 33 AD, Christ was crucified by the Romans in Jerusalem.

In 70 AD, Roman forces all but destroyed Jerusalem and had demolished the Temple. In 135 AD, the Romans rebuilt Jerusalem as the Jews lived under Roman rule. In 614 AD, the Persians had captured Jerusalem. In 629 AD, the Christians captured Jerusalem from Persians. In 638 AD, Islamic armies took it from Christians. Between 661-974 AD, Jerusalem and the Jews were under harsh Islamic rule. In 691 AD, the Muslims brazenly built their Dome of the Rock directly atop the site of the destroyed Temples. From 1099-1187 AD, Crusaders captured and ruled over the Holy City. From 1187-1259 AD, the Muslims captured Jerusalem back from the Crusaders and ruled over the Jews there.

Between 1229-1244 AD, Crusaders had recaptured Jerusalem from Muslims on two separate occasions. In 1250 AD, Muslims captured Jerusalem again, tore down the walls, and persecuted the Jewish people. During the course of the next few centuries, the Muslims nearly wiped out the Jewish population in Jerusalem. In 1516 AD, the Ottomans captured Jerusalem. Between 1538-1541 AD, the walls of Jerusalem had been rebuilt. Between 1517-1917 AD, Jews in the City lived under the rule of the Ottoman Empire. In 1917, the British captured Jerusalem in World War 1 and the Balfour Declaration was signed. The Declaration called for Jews to be able to rule over themselves in their ancient Homeland, and for Jewish people across the world to be able to return to Israel.

In 1948, the Nation of Israel was reestablished. After about 2,500 years under the rule of foreign occupiers, the Jews finally had rule over half of ancient Jerusalem and much of their original Promised Land again. In 1967, Israel recaptured the other half of Jerusalem and reunified their God-given Holy Capital. From 1967 until today, Jerusalem has been the property of Israel - never to be divided again! Hopefully, now that those of you reading know the historic connection between the Jewish State and Jerusalem, you can understand why us believers rejoiced over President Trump's Jerusalem Declaration and Embassy Move. His public recognition of the Eternal City as Israel's Capital didn't just reflect a modern reality, but recognized 5,000+ years of Jewish history.

At the end of the day, Israel needs no peace with Palestinians. The only peace Israel will ever need is that which their returning Prince of Peace can bring. Until He comes again, may the LORD continue to bless and defend Israel; because their many enemies are rising up against them. In the next chapter, I will explain just who exactly these prophesied enemies are.

THE LORD GOD OF ISRAEL HATH GIVEN REST UNTO HIS PEOPLE, THAT THEY MAY DWELL IN JERUSALEM FOR EVER.

- 1ST CHRONICLES 23:25

CHAPTER SIX

THE ENEMIES OF ISRAEL

THEY HAVE SAID, COME, AND LET US CUT THEM OFF FROM
BEING A NATION; THAT THE NAME OF ISRAEL MAY BE NO
MORE IN REMEMBRANCE.

- PSALMS 83:4

THE BIBLE PROPHESIES THAT many nations will come against
God's chosen Nation of Israel in the season leading up to Christ's
long-awaited return. Since the reestablishment of the Jewish State
in 1948, there've been numerous nations that have hated and even
wanted to destroy Israel. Though, it was not until December 21st,
2017, that we unquestionably witnessed a 2,500-year-old "Latter
Days" prophecy come to pass before our very eyes.

In the previous chapters of this book, I have explained why
Jerusalem is the God-given eternal Capital of Israel. In the Book
of Zechariah (Chapter 12 and verse 3), the prophet says, "all the
people of the earth will be gathered together *against Jerusalem*."
On that 21st day of December, the United Nations had convened
to *literally* gather together against God's Holy City. The Global
body represents all nations of Earth, and they held an emergency
session to vote on a historic anti-Israel resolution. The session
was called for by Turkey's anti-Semitic leader, President Recep
Erdogan, along with other Islamic world leaders.

They had put forth a measure condemning the United States' recognition of Jerusalem as Israel's Capital, and calling on Trump to rescind his decision to move the Embassy there. Around 200 nations had voted on the measure, and the vote would have major implications regarding "Last Days" Biblical Prophecy. It publicly determined which nations oppose Israel on the world stage, and which nations support the Jewish State. Over 75% of the world's nations went on record as being for or against God's Nation.

Anyone who carefully studies the Word of God knows that it declares Jerusalem to be the "eternal possession" of Israel nearly 1,000 times. Every single one of the nations that voted against Jerusalem being Israel's God-given property publicly opposed the LORD and welcomed His judgments. For God has said, clearly, that all nations who contend with or oppose Israel are - in reality - contending with and opposing *Him* (Isaiah 49:25). Thus, He has promised to judge, curse, and even destroy, *all nations* that come against Israel (specifically, the City of Jerusalem). 128 nations of the world set themselves up for coming destruction.

Of the 172 nations that voted, only seven (yes, just 7) voted on the side of Israel and the United States; and thus voted on the side of Almighty God. This very small number, while extremely disappointing, is actually encouraging. I believe that it may fulfill another Biblical prophecy pointing to the Rapture of the Church and the imminent return of Christ. In the Book of Micah, Chapter 5 and verse 5, we read about how the Messiah of Israel (Jesus) will be "our peace when the enemies of Israel invade the Holy Land." It goes on to say, "We will raise against them (enemies of Israel) *seven* shepherds, even *eight* commanders." An interesting connection to the UN Vote! Seven nations stood with Israel and the United States, amounting to "eight" allies of Israel in total.

The rest of the world stood *against* the LORD's people. The seven righteous nations were Guatemala, Honduras, Micronesia, the Marshall Islands, Nauru, Palau, and Togo. I'm sure that most of you reading this have probably never even heard of half these nations. Do you know who *has* heard of them, and who knows them *very well*? Almighty God. Nations of the world that we are familiar with today, the LORD is not too concerned with blessing. I speak of America's so-called allies like Canada, France, Spain, Germany, Italy, and the United Kingdom. Some of you are most likely shocked by my "God doesn't care to bless them" statement, so I will explain.

Just as all human beings have to get right with God on their own, so too, each nation of the world must put themselves on the right or wrong side of the LORD. U.S. allies that I've mentioned sided with the likes of Iran, Russia, North Korea, China, Turkey, Syria, and Saudi Arabia in the UN's Jerusalem Vote. That is *not* good company. In God's Sight, that makes some of our nation's allies just as wicked as the world's most evil regimes. America must be very careful to always remain on the side of Almighty God, as a Judeo-Christian nation, and to always support Israel.

Besides the 128 nations voting against the Jewish State, and the seven standing with Israel, 35 nations "abstained." This meant that they did not want to be on record as voting one way or the other. These are *lukewarm* nations, who are as much of a disgrace to God as the 128 nations who voted against Israel. The LORD says many times, throughout His Word, that you are either "for or against Him." There is no in the middle. There is no on the fence. You're either hot or cold. You're either a sheep or a goat. The UN vote had made clear that 163 nations of the world are completely oblivious to God's Word, and do not take His threats of judgment for opposing Israel seriously.

They're going to find out very soon just how true the Bible is, and they're going to deeply regret standing on the wrong side of history. They will all have to answer to Lord Jesus someday for their anti-Israel actions. Many people today do not realize that the main reason why He returns to Earth, in the end, is to *personally* do away with the enemies of Israel. The first time, He came to be the Messiah of Israel's eternal souls. The next time around, He'll come back down as the roaring "Lion of the Tribe of Judah" to physically fight against the wicked nations threatening the mortal lives of Israel's people. All Men and women of the earth who do not accept Jesus as the Lamb, who brings us peace with God, will someday meet Him as the Lion, who executes God's wrath.

How do YOU want to meet Him?!

The Book of Revelation is crystal clear that when all nations of the world come against Israel, to destroy the Jewish State, the armies of Heaven descend to Earth with Christ Jesus leading the charge. Before our Lord makes His descent, there are some other things concerning Israel that have to occur according to prophecy. Joel 3:2 says that nations of the world will be judged for dividing God's Holy Land. The number one goal of the UN, for nearly five decades, has been to divide up Israel's Promised Land (namely, *Jerusalem*). The United Nations is now more anti-Israel than ever before in their history, while at the same time...

- The Assad regime in Syria murders its own people.

- Iran amasses nuclear weapons to target Israel and the US.

- Islamic nations are persecuting and murdering Christians, bulldozing churches, throwing homosexuals off highrise buildings, raping children, and sexually abusing women.

- Russia continues to obtain global power by force.

Yet and still, the number one agenda of the United Nations is to target *Israel*. The UN is, no doubt, under the influence of Satan himself. According to the UNHRC (UN Human Rights Council), Israel is "the worst human rights violator in the world." No joke. I have never seen or read one news report about Christians, women, homosexuals, or Muslims, complaining about being mistreated in Israel. So, why does the UN believe the Jewish State is violating human rights *more than* China, North Korea, Russia, and Syria? Why is Israel *worse* than Islamic nations that threaten, persecute, or murder, anyone who doesn't live by their Quran? I believe it has to do with Muslim-majority nations making up a quarter of the UN's member states.

While 25% of the world may not seem like a big number, it is when they vote together on everything having to do with Israel - or should I say, everything *anti*-Israel. Every time a resolution is brought up against the Jewish State in the UN, the nearly sixty Islamic nations are guaranteed to vote against Israel - *guaranteed*. That 25% becomes a one-sided majority in UN councils, panels, and committees. As long as this remains the case, Israel will not get a fair shake in the biased UN. Throughout the past decade, the UNHRC condemned Israel more so than any of the other 192 UN member states.

There've been about 80 resolutions and decisions demonizing Israel, but only around 30 on Syria, less than 10 on North Korea - just 6 on Iran - and a whopping ZERO on Saudi Arabia, Russia, and China. Just to recap, the democratic Nation of Israel has been condemned by the UN almost *twice as much* as all of the world's most notorious and murderous regimes *combined*. As of this year, the UN Security Council has passed over 250 resolutions against Israel - more than any other nation of this world. In 2016 alone, the General Assembly adopted 20 resolutions singling out Israel - and only 3 resolutions on the rest of the world *combined*. Those 3 consisted of just one-a-piece against Iran, North Korea, and Syria.

The corrupt United Nations masquerades as an organization that promotes peace and human rights, but is nothing more than a biased body of unGodly nations that are being used by the devil to threaten God's people. In 2016, UNESCO adopted one of their most detestable anti-Israel resolutions to date. The resolution was not just an attempt to delegitimize the Jewish State, but to erase and rewrite their history. UNESCO had given Islam precedence over Judaism and Christianity, though our Faiths far outdate the "religion" of Muhammad. The resolution denied all Biblical and historical connections of the Jews to Jerusalem. The UN will now only refer to the Temple Mount and the Western Wall by Muslim titles, and no longer by their Hebrew names.

A special section of the resolution states that the sites are now "only sacred to the Islamic faith." What a blatant utter falsehood, and disgraceful denial of world history! The Temple Mount is the holiest site in Judaism, as it is believed to be where the LORD's Divine Presence is manifested more than any other place on this earth. The Bible refers to the holy hill as "Mount Zion," and it is where both Temples of the Jews had stood. The Western Wall is what remains of the second Temple. To say that neither of these sites have connection to the Jews is not only denying the Word of God, but also completely ignores 4,000+ years of human history.

The Land the UN dubs "Palestinian territory" was gifted to Israel by the LORD as an everlasting possession. Go and look up *everlasting* in the dictionary. You'll find it means eternal, endless, never-ending, and abiding forever. Do you get the picture? Well, the Biblically-illiterate UN sure doesn't! Besides the collection of anti-Israel haters in the UN, there are also specific nations of the world that are prophesied to war against the Jewish State.

One of those countries, Turkey, was the main sponsor of the 2017 Jerusalem Vote (which I opened this chapter addressing). It just so happens that Turkey is identified in the Bible as one of the nations that'll be on the front lines of the Latter-Day war against Israel. Turkey's President is one of the most anti-Semitic leaders in the world. He's publicly criticized, condemned, and threatened Israel. He hosts terror groups who are bent on Israel's destruction, and pushes anti-Israel resolutions at the UN. That explains why

President Obama was so anti-Israel. He referred to Erdogan as his "closest friend on the world stage."

Next up is Russia. Believe it or not, it is not a Muslim nation that is prophesied to lead the Islamic confederacy against Israel in the Last Days - it is Russia. The Eurasian nation, throughout the past decade, has threatened the Jewish State many times; and has allied with the exact nations that the Bible prophesied it would in the Latter Days. Earlier this year, there was a summit in Istanbul to discuss cooperation between three specific nations. The three leaders that had met and forged an unholy alliance were Erdogan of Turkey, Hassan Rouhani of Iran, and Vladimir Putin of Russia. Ezekiel 38:5-6 names Iran (Persia) and Turkey (Togarmah) as two of Russia's closest allies in its military campaign against Israel. How accurate is the Holy Bible?!

The prophecy was written over 2,500 years ago, and Russia's President (currently Vladimir Putin) is described as "Gog" in the prophecy. The war on Israel, that Putin (or whomever the leader will be at the time of the battle) leads, is called the "Gog-Magog War." *Magog* refers to ancient Magogites. They are modern-day Russians. Ezekiel also mentions the names "Rosh, Meshech, and Tubal." *Rosh* translates to Russia, *Meshech* translates to Moscow (Russia's Capital), and *Tubal* is modern Tubalsk - also located in Russia. There can be no doubt that Russia is the key player in one of the final wars against Israel.

I say "one of" the final wars, because Gog-Magog is not the same as the Battle of Armageddon. I don't want any of you to get confused when I refer to it as the "Last Days War." I believe this war will be a prelude to the war to end all wars, which is fought in and around the valley of Megiddo (which involves all nations of the world). The Gog-Magog battle is fought on the mountains of Israel, which would most likely be on the border of Syria in the Golan Heights region. I also suspect that the Islamic confederacy mentioned in Psalm 83 could be included in Gog-Magog, or they will attack Israel and fail. The latter scenario would surely lead to Russia entering the battle as the chief military leader.

It is no wonder that Russia is prophesied to be the strongest military power in the Last Days, because Vladimir Putin's regime currently possesses the most nuclear weapons in the world today - even more than the United States of America. As of 2017, Russia had approximately 2,000 nuclear warheads deployed. Thanks be to God that even one-million nuclear bombs are powerless against Israel's ultimate Defense Force: the LORD God Almighty.

One of the closest allies of Russia on the world stage today, and undoubtedly the number one modern enemy of Israel, is Iran. The Ayatollahs of Iran have been itching to go to war with Israel for decades. The Islamic regime's leaders have long threatened to "blow Israel off the map." The supreme leader of Iran, Ayatollah Khameni, had revealed in a televised speech that Iran's reason for participating in the 2015 "Nuclear Deal" with world powers was "*not* for eventual peace." He said that the long drawn out talks had instead been an opportunity to build up his nation's nuclear arsenal to use against Israel "*soon*."

Iran's so-called moderate President, Hassan Rouhani, has also publicly called for the "destruction of Israel." Even after he had signed the horrible Nuclear Deal with Obama and world leaders, both Rouhani and Khameni had chanted "death to America" and "death to Israel" on live TV. The Book of Ezekiel says "Persia" (modern-day Iran) will be one of the most threatening enemies of Israel in the Last Days. Another prophecy about Iran, also found in Ezekiel (32:24), has come to pass in our day. The prophet said that the nation would be an exporter of *terror*. The Islamic regime in Tehran is the biggest funder and organizer of terror worldwide, especially against Israel.

Finally, no document regarding the enemies of Israel could be complete without mention of Palestine. The Jewish State's hostile neighbor has been a constant thorn in Israel's side; and not just through terrorism, but in the United Nations as well - where they dirty Israel's good name in the realm of public opinion. Year after year, Palestinian leadership has tried to influence world leaders to support and aid their cause against the Jewish State. They have long sought, through UN pressure or even force, to take some of Israel's God-given Land as their own. I allude to this subject of "Land-for-Peace" in the previous Israel chapters, and I will again in the "Extreme Weather" chapter.

Gaza in Palestine is the home base of the terror group *Hamas*. They're responsible for murdering thousands of innocent Israelis, many of whom have been women and children. In 2014, they had fired 5,000+ rockets into Israel. Yet, the global mainstream media demonized the Jewish State for retaliating against those so-called "poor Palestinians." How many other nations of the world would just sit on their hands when 5,000 missiles were being fired across their border? The short answer is *none*. Still, the world always urges Israel to show restraint against terrorists. It's unbelievable.

In early 2018, as Israelis were preparing for celebrations of the 70th Anniversary of their Nation's rebirth, Hamas was staging an attempted invasion of Israel's border with Gaza. While Hamas was telling the global media that the Palestinians were preparing to hold "peaceful protests" along Israel's border fence, they were - at the same time - telling the Palestinian people to prepare for "the beginning of the capturing all of Israel." The Spokesman for Palestinian President Mahmoud Abbas had reiterated Hamas' *real* reason for organizing the protests (which were really riots) - "The message of our people is clear: Israel will be *removed*."

At the same time these threats against the Jewish State were being made by Palestinian leaders, under the guise of "peaceful" protests, the lamestream media was selling the narrative (as they always do) that Israel was the *aggressor* and that the Palestinians were "poor and defenseless protesters" under fire. Nothing, and I mean *absolutely nothing*, could be any further from the truth. For six weeks, tens of thousands of Palestinians had stormed Israel's border - rolling burning tires toward the security fence - throwing grenades, molotov cocktails, pipe bombs, rocks, bricks, and axes. They brandished guns, machetes, and wire cutters for the fence: and flew flaming kites over the border to start fires in Israel.

The Palestinians who were killed by Israeli forces for rushing the border fence, in an attempt to breach it, had all been carrying weapons. They were mostly all card-carrying members of Hamas. Of course, the media conveniently left that out - simply running headlines that read: "Israel kills dozens of Palestinians." I could write a whole 'nother book about why today's biased mainstream media is one of the biggest enemies of Israel. The media should be ashamed of their one-sided reporting, and for trying to deceive ignorant audiences to believe their biased narrative. They portray Israel as the "bad guy," and the Palestinian terrorists as the "good guys." Exactly what kind of alternate reality do the liberal media journalists live in anyway?

The term gets tossed around a lot today, but when it comes to reporting on the Israeli-Palestinian conflict, the mainstream media is full of *fake news*. Besides the nations I have already mentioned, Israel is preparing for possible wars with every bordering nation. I've already addressed Hamas on the South-Southwest border in Gaza. They are in league with another Palestinian terrorist group known as Islamic Jihad. On the Northern border, there is Lebanon - home to the Iran-backed Hezbollah terror group. In 2006, they fired around 4,000 rockets into the Jewish State. On the Northeast border, there is Syria and ISIS - and neither of them are fond of Israel. On the Eastern border, there is Jordan. The country's King, Abdullah, is anti-Semitic and anti-Israel to the core.

The tiny Jewish Nation is surrounded by much larger hostile enemies on every side. Yet, those nations have never succeeded in their quests to destroy Israel. And the number one reason for their constant failure is that Almighty God dwells *in the midst of* Israel, as their eternal Defender (Joel 2:27). In the end, though virtually the whole world comes against them, *Israel wins*. They will win, because *God wins*. The LORD's always been, still is, and forever will be, fighting on their behalf. HalleluYah to the God of Israel!

AND IT SHALL COME TO PASS IN THAT DAY, THAT I WILL SEEK
TO DESTROY ALL THE NATIONS THAT COME AGAINST
JERUSALEM, SAITH THE LORD.

- ZECHARIAH 12:9

CHAPTER SEVEN

SIGNS IN THE HEAVENS

I WILL SHEW WONDERS IN THE HEAVENS... THE SUN SHALL BE
TURNED INTO DARKNESS, AND THE MOON INTO BLOOD,
BEFORE THE GREAT AND NOTABLE DAY OF THE LORD COME.

- ACTS 2:19-20 & JOEL 2:30-31

OUR GENERATION HAS SEEN, quite possibly, far more signs
in the heavens than any other since Christ ascended into Heaven
about 2,000 years ago. It's undeniable that God has been trying to
get our attention. Between 2014-2018, we observed an abundance
of extremely rare and historic occurrences in the Sun, the Moon,
and our skies in general. After reading this compelling chapter, it
is my hope that you'll find it very difficult to not be enthusiastic
about the coming Rapture of the Church.

During the years 2014-2015, we had witnessed the very rare
occurrence of a *Blood Moon Tetrad*. Four Blood Moons had risen
directly on Biblical Feast Days. Try chalking that up to just mere
coincidence. Two years in a row, we observed 2 of them rise on
the Feast of Passover; while the other 2 occurred during the Feast
of Tabernacles. If a pair of Blood Moons transpired during God's
Holy Feasts in one year, that would be intriguing enough in itself.
The fact that this happened two years in a row is unprecedented,
and it is beyond fascinating.

That's not all though... 2 of the 4 Blood Moons occurred in the Biblical *Shemitah Year*. The Shemitah Year only occurs once every seven years. Moreover, that particular Shemitah was what is known as a *Super Shemitah* - meaning it was the 7th Shemitah in a cycle of seven! How can even the most hardened Bible skeptics write off, as a coincidence, Blood Moons rising on Biblical Holy Days AND during the all-important 7th Shemitah in a set of 7?! The Biblical Year which followed the Super Shemitah was known as the *Jubilee Year*. The Jubilee only comes around once every 50 years! We had seen the final Blood Moon of the Tetrad rise in the Jubilee Year of 2015.

All of this is so extremely important, concerning the return of Jesus Christ, because it has all taken place in the generation that witnessed the rebirth of Israel. As I've explained in the "Fig Tree" chapter, none of the "Last Days" signs given in the Bible could mean anything until the Nation of Israel was reestablished. While there have always been Blood Moons, Solar Eclipses, and other signs in the heavens throughout history, they have had nothing to do with End Times Prophecy. Those occurring in our generation have absolutely *everything* to do with it.

If I ended this chapter here, I believe this should be enough to strengthen the faith of even the most backslidden of believers - but I'm far from done. In 2016, again on the Feast of Tabernacles, God had ushered in His Holy Week with a sign in the heavens. A Supermoon had risen. The celestial event occurs when the Moon makes its closest approach to Earth. 2016's Supermoon had come to its second nearest position to Planet Earth since 1948 (222,365 miles), behind only the Supermoon to fall just a month later. One night earlier, on the eve of the Biblical Feast, a *Super Blood Moon* rose! Remember the significance of 1948? Keep the year in mind as we go further, as it is beyond important prophetically.

The second Supermoon of 2016 was the closest the Moon has been to Earth in this *century*. It will not be that close again until the fall of 2034. The closest Full Moon of the 21st century will not rise until the winter of 2052! The year in which we witnessed the two historic Supermoons, while being 2016 on our Gregorian calendar, was the year 5777 on the Hebrew calendar. In the "Fig Tree" chapter, I'd explained why 777 is the number of Almighty God (YHWH) the God of Israel. Speaking of Israel, the reason I told you to remember the year 1948 was because it was the year that the Nation of Israel was officially reborn! So, the Supermoon of 5777 was the largest and the brightest it has ever been since the fulfilled prophecy of the Jewish State's rebirth.

If you are not saying *WOW* yet, you aren't paying attention. In chapter 4, I had also mentioned that God "appointed the Moon for seasons." Given all of the recent signs in the Moon, I believe we are living in *the season* of something historic prophetically. Could it really be the Rapture? Maybe a Biblical War? A historic disaster? Global government? All I know for certain is that the LORD is using the Moon to alert us to something coming; and as I've previously said, I wholeheartedly believe that the *something* is really a *Someone*.

In Luke, Chapter 21 and verse 25, Lord Jesus prophesied that "There shall be signs in the Sun, and the Moon, and the stars." In verse 27, He said, "*Then* shall they see the Son of man coming in a cloud with power and great glory." Notice He also mentioned the Sun. Most Biblical prophecies about the Sun reveal it "will be darkened." This, to me, signifies a *Total Solar Eclipse*. Now, of course, there've been thousands of Eclipses of the Sun throughout history; because of this, some people tend to ignore the prophetic significance of Solar Eclipses. They are wrong to do so. As I've already explained, none of His signs could mean anything until 1948. That began the time frame to start paying closer attention to the Moon and the Sun.

Just last year, America had experienced its first coast-to-coast Total Solar Eclipse in 99 years. That is extremely significant, as it would be the first our nation has seen since the Jews reclaimed their ancient Holy Land. It was also the first Total Eclipse of the Sun since 1979. I wasn't even born yet! So it has definitely been awhile. To say that it was a rare occurrence of the Sun would be an understatement. On August 21st of 2017, in the middle of the day, skies were darkened from one American coast to the other. The Moon passed between the Sun and Earth, blocking the face of the Sun and leaving only its corona visible in the sky. All of North America had experienced at least a partial Eclipse.

The difference between a full and a partial Eclipse is literally the difference between night and day. During a Total Eclipse, the temps drop and the horizon is ringed by colors of sunset. The sky becomes a twilight blue, and stars and planets become visible in the middle of the day. The Eclipse moved over a dozen States, occurring at the end of the Biblical month of Av - right before the start of Elul, which is known as the "month of repentance." What is even more important, is it occurred in the significant year 5777.

I had found it thought-provoking that the path of the Eclipse had drawn a line directly through the *heartland* of America. This is noteworthy; because President Donald Trump, at the time, was following in the Obama administration's footsteps in attempting to forge a Peace Deal between the Israelis and Palestinians. Any deal between the two parties would unquestionably divide up the Holy Land of Israel (the *Heartland* of God). In previous chapters, I mentioned that the division of Israel's God-given Land is what causes the LORD to pour out His Wrath upon the nations (Joel 3:2). If our country has any role in the division of God's Holy Land, we can be sure that God will *divide America.*

So, it was no surprise that as President Trump was pushing hard for Israel to give up "Land-for-peace" to Palestine, God used the Eclipse to *literally* draw a line through the *heart* of America. It was no coincidence that this warning to America came during the 50th Anniversary of Israel reunifying Jerusalem. In virtually every Land-for-Peace Deal that U.S. Presidents have drawn up for Israel and Palestine, chunks of Jerusalem have been on the table. This absolutely infuriates the LORD.

I was fascinated when I found that the Eclipse had more than a few connections to the Holy City. I had discovered that the first major American city to witness the Total Eclipse was the Capital of Oregon, which is SALEM. For those of you who are unaware, Salem is the original Biblical Name for Jerusalem. God's beloved City was first known as Salem in the days of Melchizedek, and it was first referred to in Genesis, Chapter 14. In another instance that was hardly coincidence, there were 14 States in the totality line of the Eclipse. Genesis 14 and 14 States. Pretty awesome if you ask me! Also, out of the 14 States that could view the Eclipse in totality, 13 of them had cities named *Salem*. Google it, so you can see that I'm not just cooking this stuff up in my head.

Those 13 States were Georgia, Idaho, Illinois, Iowa, Kansas, Kentucky, Missouri, Montana, Nebraska, North Carolina, Oregon, South Carolina, and Tennessee. The only State that did not have a city named Salem was Wyoming, but there is a city in Wyoming named *Homa Hills*; and there is a Hill in Israel named *Har Homa*. Israel's Har Homa just so happens to be located in JERUSALEM. Also, seven years from that Eclipse, another Total Solar Eclipse will pass over the United States of America (in 2024). The 2024 Eclipse will cross directly over the line of the previous Eclipse's path, forming an X. When two Eclipse paths cross, there can only be one singular point on the earth where both centerlines meet. So, literally, X marks the spot.

The centerlines of the two Eclipses will meet near the eastern shore of Cedar Lake in Illinois. If you were to zoom in on a map, you will get goosebumps. Believe it or not, the closest road to the point where the two Eclipses intersect is SALEM Road. What are the odds?! It's also important to note that two Total Solar Eclipses occurring exactly seven years apart is really rare. A Total Solar

Eclipse can only be seen from the same place on Earth once every 375 years. I think God is sending a message to U.S. leadership through the Eclipse, saying, "Hands off My Holy Land!"

Sadly, Trump's administration seemed to ignore the warning, and continued forcing Israel back to the negotiating table with the Palestinians. During the month after the Eclipse, Jared Kushner (the President's son-in-law) flew to Israel to meet with the Israeli and Palestinian leaders to discuss a Peace Deal. In the same hours that he did, one of the most powerful hurricanes to ever strike America - Harvey - had devastated the Southeast.

In January of 2018, for the first time since March of 1866, an extraordinarily rare *Blue Super Blood Moon* had appeared in the heavens. The trifecta event combined a Blue Moon, a Supermoon, and a Blood Moon (Total Lunar Eclipse) all-in-one. Though the saying "once in a Blue Moon" would imply that it's rare, the Blue Moon is actually quite common. What is extremely uncommon is when it's combined with a Blood Moon *and* a Supermoon. To put it into perspective, the last time that these three celestial events occurred in conjunction with one another was 200 years ago.

Besides these rare occurrences in the heavenly bodies, there's been another sign taking place in the skies above - trumpet-like sounds and mysterious booms have emanated from the heavens for much of the past decade. These unexplained noises have been heard all around the world. They purportedly began in 2008, but became much more widespread in 2011. The sounds have baffled meteorologists, geologists, NASA, authorities, and governments. The trumpet sounds have become a global phenomenon. I have watched many videos chronicling them, from around the globe, and they all sound exactly like a shofar being blown.

For those not aware, a shofar is a ram's horn that was used by ancient Israel to call assemblies, prepare for battle, or to signal a Holy Feast beginning. The shofar is referred to as a trumpet in the Bible. The trumpet sounds coming from our skies should be an obvious "Last Days" sign for believers everywhere. There are so many verses in God's Word that declare the sounding of heavenly trumpets as a precursor to the Rapture and as heralding judgments during the 7-year Tribulation. Trumpets are mentioned numerous times in the Book of Revelation. The fact they are mysteriously being heard from the heavens, all across this world, should have believers shaping up, looking up, and packing up, because I truly believe that we will be *going up* real soon!

AND HE SHALL SEND HIS ANGELS WITH A GREAT SOUND OF A TRUMPET, AND THEY SHALL GATHER TOGETHER HIS ELECT... FROM ONE END OF HEAVEN TO THE OTHER.

- MATTHEW 24:31

CHAPTER EIGHT

EARTHQUAKES & EXTREME WEATHER

THERE SHALL BE GREAT EARTHQUAKES IN DIVERS PLACES.

- LUKE 21:11/MATTHEW 24:7/MARK 13:8

THERE ARE MANY SCOFFERS of the Holy Bible, and of Bible Prophecy in particular, who love to say that "we have *always* had powerful earthquakes." What they fail to realize, as I have pointed out in the previous chapters, is that none of the world's strongest quakes could have meant anything regarding End Times Prophecy until 1948. That, of course, was the year that the Nation of Israel reappeared on the world scene. The existence of the Jewish State is absolutely central to the return of Christ. With that in mind, I'm sure the scoffers would be surprised to learn that 7 out of the 10 most powerful earthquakes of the past 400 years have come *after* 1948. 70% occurred in *our generation.*

On top of that, 5 out of the 7 magnitude 9.0 or higher quakes have occurred after 1948. Again... over 70%. I think it is obvious that this generation has seen an uptick in powerful quakes. The largest temblor ever recorded, 9.5 on the Richter scale, devastated Chile in 1960. So, the most powerful earthquake on record shook the earth *after 1948*. Actually, the top 5 most massive earthquakes had all come after '48 - Chile (9.5 in 1960), Alaska (9.2 in 1964), Sumatra (9.1 in 2004), Kamchatka (9.0 in 1952), and Japan (9.0

in 2011). Just one year before the historic Japan earthquake and ensuing tsunami, in 2010, Chile had been rocked by a destructive 8.8 magnitude temblor.

Since the year 2000, there have been about 275 earthquakes of magnitude 7.0 or higher. Earthquakes above 6.0 magnitude are considered "strong," while those at or above the 7.0 threshold are dubbed "powerful." Obviously, anything above an 8.0 is referred to as "great." In less than two decades, the world has experienced nearly 300 of the quakes that Jesus prophesied would occur in the *Last Days* leading up to His imminent return.

In the last chapter, I had written about the Supermoon of the Century. On the eve of that historic sign in the heavens, there was a massive 7.8 magnitude quake that rocked New Zealand. In the news reports, the New Zealand city dominating the headlines was CHRISTCHURCH. Students of Bible Prophecy strongly believe that the Rapture of Christ's Church is ever on the horizon. That's the reason I'm writing this! God may have been giving sleeping believers a wake-up call. In the Hebrew Year 5777, on the eve of the historic Supermoon, "ChristChurch" topped the headlines of every major news source in the world! How can we not be eagerly looking up, and listening for our Lord to say "come up hither"?!

Now, before I address the hurricanes, I would be remiss not to mention California when talking about powerful earthquakes. In recent years, there has been an increase of quake activity along America's West Coast. This has many believing that the next "Big One" in the world may very well strike the USA. A recent study had concluded that, in the very near future, the 800-mile-long San Andreas fault could unzip all at once. The fault runs the length of California, where the Pacific and North American plates meet. It was long thought that it could only rupture in isolated sections. But the study by federal, state, and academic researchers showed much of the fault could rupture all at once - which would unleash a devastating historic catastrophe.

Top geological experts all believe the fault is way overdue for a *massive* earthquake. If you're a believer in Cali, I'd be praying for the Lord's protection over your property and family. If you are anywhere near the San Andreas fault, I would highly recommend that you *move*. California is one of the most Godless States in our union today, so they're due for judgment, and believers should get out while they can. Speaking of judgment, I'd now like to focus on the historic hurricanes that the world has experienced in recent memory and how they relate to Scripture.

As with earthquakes, economic collapse, tornado outbreaks, and wildfires, I think the hurricanes are a form of God's judgment upon a nation. The biggest reason for His Wrath being poured out upon nations is mistreatment of Israel. That mistreatment entails leaders of a nation pressuring the Jewish State to give up some of their eternal God-given Land for potential peace with their hostile neighbors in Palestine. In this chapter, I will connect some of the strongest, costliest, most destructive, and deadliest hurricanes in American history to our leaders attempting to broker the division of Israel's Holy Land. While there've indeed been many reasons throughout the past few decades that the USA has given God to judge our nation, forcing Israel into lopsided Peace Deals in favor of the terrorist Palestinians takes the cake.

Other reasons for incurring His wrath are removing Him from our government and the public square, moral decay, widespread blasphemy, legalization of sins (such as Gay Marriage), and the holocaust of babies through abortion. 21st century America has given God *far too many* reasons. Our country was founded as a Judeo-Christian Nation; and there can be no argument that when this country departs from its Godly foundation, it certainly suffers the consequences.

The list of names for the 2018 Atlantic Hurricane Season was recently released, and I'd advised fellow believers to take note of them. Let me be clear, I don't claim to be a "prophet." I simply observe the signs of the times occurring all around us through a Biblical lens. I don't follow a majority of the world in attributing the record-breaking weather events to random climate change or global warming. The connections of so many U.S. disasters to the mistreatment of Israel, alone, should convince the most hardened skeptics that the Hand of our God is truly at work in the weather.

The reason I tell believers to pay close attention to the names of hurricanes is because the LORD is well aware of the names on every year's list. If history is any proof, I believe He specifically uses Biblically-named storms to leave no doubt that they are His judgments. After I observed the 2018 List, I counted five Biblical names, and they were:

1. Debby (*Deborah*)
2. Isaac
3. Michael
4. Rafael (*Raphael*)
5. Sara (*Sarah/Sarai*)

Anyone familiar with the Bible will clearly recognize these names. Two of them (Michael and Raphael) are Archangels, and the other three are well-known Old Testament names. To prove the significance of Biblically-named hurricanes, I researched the list of all retired U.S. hurricanes. In 1953, the storms began being named. Originally, only female names had been used for tropical cyclones. The World Meteorological Organization added the male names in 1979. Storms causing the most devastation were deemed significant enough to have their names retired. It's no coincidence that the very first male hurricane name to be retired was *Biblical*. That 1979 hurricane was named DAVID, which was the name of God's beloved King of ancient Israel.

David was a historic Category 5 hurricane. With winds of 175 mph, the storm had left widespread damage in its wake - costing

$320-million (nearly one-*billion* dollars today). It was the first - and the last - use of the name David, being immediately retired following the storm because of its devastation and high death toll. What I had found extremely interesting, while viewing an image of the hurricane making landfall in the United States, was that it looked to me like a map of the modern-day Nation of Israel. Sure enough, after downloading a map of Israel and superimposing the storm image over it, it seemed to fit perfectly. Coincidence? I do not think you can believe in coincidence or chance, while also believing in God. Everything happens for a reason with Him.

The fact that the first ever male-named hurricane to be retired was David (King of Israel), and the storm had actually mirrored the shape of the modern-day State of Israel, is beyond captivating. Prepare to be fascinated even more by the connection between the hurricane and the U.S. brokering a deal in which Israel had been pressured to give up "Land-for-peace" to their hostile neighbors. On March 26th, 1979, a Peace Treaty was signed between Israel and Egypt *on American soil*. It was witnessed by U.S. President Jimmy Carter in Washington. The Treaty required the complete withdrawal by Israelis from the Sinai Peninsula, which the Jewish State captured during the Six-Day War of 1967.

On August 25th, 1979, the eve of the 6-month anniversary of the treaty signing, Hurricane David formed. This was one of the first of many examples showing God's extreme displeasure with America pushing Israel to give up chunks of their Promised Land for so-called "peace." The first retired Biblically-named female Hurricane I discovered, that was also associated with Israel, was BEULAH. While David was an obvious Biblical name that even unbelievers are familiar with, Beulah is a name familiar only to well-studied Bible students. The name is used in Isaiah, Chapter 6 and verse 4, where God says the Jews will reinhabit their ancient God-given Land. He tells them that they are *married* to the Land of Israel. Beulah, in the Hebrew, means "married."

It is extremely interesting to note that Hurricane Beulah had struck America in the year 1967. Beulah formed exactly 3 months *to-the-day* of June 5th, which just so happened to be the start of Israel's 6-Day War with their aggressive Muslim neighbors. That was the miraculous war in which Israel defeated the many Arab nations coming against the Jewish State to destroy her, and when they had reclaimed much of their ancient Homeland. Two of the most important pieces of the Promised Land that Israel reacquired in the war were Eastern Jerusalem and Judea. So, the LORD had fulfilled the ancient Biblical prophecy of Isaiah, that contained the name "Beulah," three months to-the-day of the storm forming!

Also, it is important to note that leading up to the Six-Day War, American leadership had refused Israeli requests for military aid. The U.S. also refused to approve an Israeli preemptive attack on Egypt, even though the Jewish State's enemies were preparing to launch an attack against her on all sides. Could Beulah have been Almighty God's rebuke to the USA for not defending His chosen Nation? I can't possibly be the first one to ever notice this, can I?! This was nothing short of the Hand of God at work.

Beulah was the strongest, and the only, major hurricane of the 1967 Atlantic Hurricane Season. It, like David, was a devastating Category 5 storm. It spawned 115 tornadoes across Texas, which had established a new record for the highest amount of tornadoes ever produced by a tropical cyclone. Due to slow movement over Texas, Beulah led to significant flooding and the total damage had reached $235-million (that is over $800-million dollars today). It is greatly symbolic that Texas was the State which God chose to bring His wrath upon, as it's called the "Lone Star State." There is another place known as a *Lone Star State* in the world today, and that would be the Nation of ISRAEL.

The next retired Biblical name I came across was ANDREW, who was one of our Lord Jesus' disciples. For those of you not well-studied in the disciples, Andrew and his brother Peter were the two whom Jesus said that He would make "fishers of men." In August 1992, Andrew became a disastrous Category 5 hurricane. It was the most powerful hurricane to ever hit the State of Florida until 2017's Irma. It was also the costliest hurricane to ever make landfall in America until Katrina in 2005. It is the 7th costliest hurricane in U.S. history, and caused over $27-*billion* in damage. I am sure you're wondering if Andrew was also connected to the mistreatment of Israel? The answer would be yes.

On the 23rd of August, President George H.W. Bush held his second Madrid Conference which had pressured Israel to give up "Land-for-peace" to Palestinians. On the very *same day*, Andrew made landfall in Florida. At that time, the hurricane was the worst natural disaster to ever hit America. Just a few years ago, another disciple made the list of Biblically-named retired hurricanes - and that was MATTHEW. Hurricane Matthew was the first Category 5 Atlantic hurricane since Felix in 2007. The destructive storm had caused widespread damage in Haiti, and in the Southeastern United States. It was the deadliest Atlantic hurricane since Stan in 2005. In Florida, over one-million homes lost power, and damage from Matthew across the United States reached about $10-*billion*.

The storm made landfall in the U.S. during the *same week* of the Feast of Trumpets, also known as Rosh Hashana. Moreover, the hurricane formed in the Atlantic on September 24th. That's so Biblically significant. Matthew's Gospel, Chapter 24, is regarded among Prophecy buffs as one of the most important portions of Scripture pertaining to signs of Jesus Christ's return. Aside from Revelation, Mark (Chapter 13), and Luke (Chapter 21), Matthew 24 gives us Jesus' firsthand account of the signs we are to watch for pointing to the Rapture and His Second Coming. The fact that Matthew had formed on the 24th, during the *High Holy Days*, is not just interesting... but it is simply *incredible*.

The final and most recent Biblically-named retired hurricane you should all be very familiar with, as it occurred in 2017. It was

MARIA, the 3rd most costliest Atlantic hurricane in U.S. history. For those unaware, Maria is the translation in many languages for the name of *Mary*. Everyone on planet Earth should know Mary was the Virgin Mother of our Lord Jesus. Just like the hurricane bearing the name of globally recognizable King David, the storm bearing Mary's name will be remembered for a long time. Maria, also a powerful Category 5, had become the worst natural disaster on record in Dominica and Puerto Rico - and 10th most intense Atlantic hurricane ever recorded. Total damages are estimated to be close to $100-*billion*.

Much like the other historic Cat-5 hurricanes that have struck the U.S., Maria was connected to our leadership demanding that Israelis give up some of their Land for "peace" with Palestinians. The devastating storm had made landfall in the U.S. territory of Puerto Rico on the eve of the Feast of Trumpets (also New Year's Day in Israel). It was the third, and the final, major hurricane to strike real estate of the USA in just a month's time - following Harvey and Irma. The three Category 4 and 5 storms striking that close together was unprecedented to my knowledge. Even more astounding, all three back-to-back-to-back devastating hurricanes struck at the end of the Biblical year 5777. All three of them had made the list of the Top 5 Costliest U.S. Hurricanes on record.

I also believe that the three of them hitting in close succession symbolized the Trinity (the Father, Son, and Holy Spirit) warning U.S. leadership to "*back off Israel.*" I say this, because the trifecta of hurricanes struck our nation immediately following the Trump administration restarting the Israeli-Palestinian Peace Process. It was in the same day - even the *same hours* - that their delegation had met with Israeli Prime Minister Netanyahu and Palestinian President Abbas to renew the Mideast Peace Talks, when the first major hurricane to hit Texas in twelve years had formed; and that record-shattering hurricane was known as Harvey.

It was the longest a Texas hurricane remained a named storm after landfall since 1971. The storm had poured out the greatest amount of rain ever recorded in the Lower 48 States from a single storm. Nearly 30-*trillion* gallons of rain had fallen on Texas and Louisiana over a six-day period - enough to fill Texas' Houston Astrodome 85,000 times. In less than a week! WOW. Think about that. Harvey became the 2nd most expensive storm in American history, at around $125-*billion*, behind only Katrina. Harvey was also the first Cat-4 storm to make landfall in the U.S. in almost 15 years. While the hurricane was still wreaking havoc on the Lone Star State, and its surrounding states, another monster storm was forming in the Atlantic - Irma.

Sadly, the POTUS didn't learn from Harvey to stop pushing "Land-for-Peace" on Israel. Trump would meet with Netanyahu and Abbas on the sidelines of the UN General Assembly in New York. His administration had said that the meetings would focus specifically on "laying a foundation" for the Peace Process, which would include Israeli Land on the negotiating table. Irma, another Category 4 hurricane, made landfall in the U.S. on the first day of the week that Trump held the meetings. Irma became one of the strongest storms ever recorded, packing 185 mph winds before it struck America. It was the first storm ever observed, in any ocean, to sustain winds of 185 mph for more than 24 hours. Irma had maintained 185 mph for 37 straight hours.

The storm's arrival in Florida, following Harvey, marked the first time on record that two Category 4 Hurricanes made landfall in the USA during the same year. Hurricane Irma had generated enough accumulated cyclone energy to meet NOAA's definition of a *full* Atlantic Hurricane Season. Also, by itself, Irma had been more powerful than 18 of 51 full Hurricane Seasons since 1966. That mammoth storm blanketed the entire State of Florida, and had impacted surrounding states with hurricane-force winds and record flooding. There have also been some other historic storms and hurricanes striking the USA, connected to America forcing Israel into Land-for-Peace Deals, that were not Biblically-named.

Back on October 31st of 1991, George H.W. Bush promoted his first Madrid Peace Conference - in which he sought to divide up the Land of Israel in exchange for peace with the Palestinians. On the very *next day*, what would become known as "the Perfect Storm" had formed in the Atlantic. The rare storm moved east to west, as opposed to a natural track from west to east. The storm was so unusual that a book and a movie had been made about it. President Bush's home and his vacation compound were severely damaged by the storm. Waves as high as his 3-story home filled the house with sea water, and had caused extensive damage.

On September 13th, 1993, President Bill Clinton signed the "Oslo Accord," labeled a "Land-for-Peace" accord that demanded Israel give away some of their Holy Land to the Palestinians. The very *next day*, Hurricane Emily would slam into the United States with winds up to 115 miles per hour.

On September 28th, 1998, while Secretary of State Albright was finishing up final details of an agreement that required Israel surrender 13% of Judea and Samaria to the Palestinians, President Clinton met with Palestinian President Yasser Arafat and Israeli Prime Minister Benjamin Netanyahu at the White House. As he briefed them on the agreement, Hurricane George had blasted the Gulf Coast with 110 mph winds and gusts up to 175 mph. The storm caused $1-*billion* in damage. It was at the exact time when Arafat departed U.S. soil that the storm began to dissipate.

In 2005, Hurricane Katrina formed on the *same exact day* that Israel was being forced by President George W. Bush, through his *Roadmap to Peace,* to finalize forcibly evacuating thousands of Jews from their homes in the Gaza Strip. In a mirror image, at the *same time* that the Jews were being forced out of their homes in Gaza, thousands of Americans in the South were being evacuated from their cities and towns due to Katrina's flooding.

Back to present-day... It was announced in early 2018 that the Trump Peace Plan would be unveiled after the Embassy move to Israel's Capital of Jerusalem. The Embassy event took place on May 14th, the 70th Anniversary of Israel's rebirth. There've been reports (and I pray they are false) that the President's upcoming plan would call for Israel to hand over 40% of Judea and Samaria to the Palestinians. Not to mention, parts of Jerusalem. There are some reports indicating that the Old City of Jerusalem could be internationalized! That sounds like something the United Nations has been calling for, and it would *not* sit well with God. If these reports are true, America had better prepare for another historic hurricane striking the nation again real soon.

Hurricanes are not the only extreme weather that the world has been contending with in recent years. There has been extreme heat across the globe. 2016 was the warmest year on record since record-keeping began in the 1800s. The heat record was recently broken 3 years in a row, according to NOAA (National Oceanic and Atmospheric Administration). 16 of the 17 hottest years have occurred since the year 2000, and 2017 was the third hottest year on record. As many of you know, the Godless liberals have been pushing the "global warming" theory - that *man* is responsible for the increase in temperature instead of God controlling it. As with theories of evolution and the Big Bang, global warming theorists desire to eliminate God from the picture.

Newsflash to everyone reading this: "man" has no power over the weather. Our actions cannot influence it in any way except for *one*. The only way we can ever influence the conditions on Earth is through our *sin*. Hear what God says in Isaiah, Chapter 24 and verses 5-6 -

"THE EARTH ALSO IS DEFILED UNDER THE INHABITANTS THEREOF; BECAUSE THEY HAVE TRANSGRESSED THE LAWS, CHANGED THE ORDINANCE, BROKEN THE EVERLASTING COVENANT. THEREFORE HATH THE CURSE DEVOURED THE

EARTH, AND THEY THAT DWELL THEREIN ARE DESOLATE: THEREFORE THE INHABITANTS OF THE EARTH ARE BURNED, AND FEW MEN LEFT."

The LORD says that our sins bring a curse upon the earth, and one of the effects of that is inhabitants of Earth being burned with "great heat" (Revelation 16:9). Also, for the theory of global warming to be true, Earth would have to continue to get hotter year after year. That was not the case in 2018. We went from the 3rd hottest year on record in 2017, to one of the coldest winters in over a century. In Southern Michigan, where I'm from, only the winter of 2000-01 had been colder than the 2017-18 season over the course of the past century. Enduring such a miserable freezing winter, which was also the longest since the 1800s, has led me to believe we're experiencing *global cooling* - not global warming!

Michigan wasn't alone, as hundreds of millions of Americans had suffered under record-low temperatures this past winter. 2017 saw the coldest first week of any winter on record for dozens of cities in the East. The New Year's Eve ball drop in NYC's Times Square took place amid the coldest weather in half-a-century. The midnight temp was only 10 degrees above zero, with a wind chill of -5 to -20 degrees below zero. Numerous record lows had been set across the United States, throughout December and January, and wind chills in the 50s below zero were recorded. The deep freeze wasn't just occurring in the U.S. either. In my research, I discovered that Bangladesh, Russia, South Korea, and U.K. had endured record-cold temperatures during the winter of 2017-18.

Rollercoaster weather changes, from extreme hot to extreme cold, can only ever be explained by Someone controlling it. The theories of global warming and climate change cannot explain the seesaw weather we've recently been experiencing. The only thing that has ever made sense of it, for thousands of years, is the Word of God. Why is it so far-fetched to believe that the Creator of the

Universe, Creator of everything that is seen and unseen, controls our weather? His Word is clear He does. Every verse I could find pertaining to weather starts with the words "He brings, He causes, He commands, He creates, He gives, He makes, and He sends."

Notice that *not once* does the Holy Bible ever use the phrases "man causes" or "man makes" when speaking of weather on the earth. This means the theory of climate change is incompatible with Almighty God's Word. No Christian or Jew should embrace the theory, which is forcefully pushed upon the world as truth. It most certainly is not. The climate change/global warming agenda discourages belief in the *real* truth, which is God's Eternal Word. Men and women of influence, like former U.S. President Obama, uber-liberal Pope Francis, Al Gore, and atheist scientist Bill Nye, all push the false narrative that "man can make the weather" - and that man can take steps to "change the weather." This widely held belief denies our God, by replacing the Creator with the creation.

This fulfills a "Last Days" prophecy of Saint Paul in Romans, Chapter 1 and verse 25 –

"THEY CHANGED THE TRUTH OF GOD INTO A LIE, AND WORSHIPPED AND SERVED THE CREATION MORE THAN THE CREATOR, WHO IS BLESSED FOREVER."

I believe this verse also condemns those worshiping the earth, spending their whole lives trying to *save it* - while the Holy Bible is clear that God will fix it in the end. If this generation actually read their Bibles, they'd know that. We need to focus our short time in this world on getting *souls* saved. Let God take care of saving the earth, because only *He* can. Proverbs, Chapter 11 and verse 30, teaches us that "He that winneth souls is wise." Yet, the far-left Scientific community and our day and age's *great thinkers* like to call climate change deniers uneducated simpletons, whose beliefs are archaic. I don't know about you, but I'd rather believe and do things God teaches are wise - instead of going along with the crowd, to be celebrated as a progressive man of the world.

I'll never apologize, nor be shamed by anyone, for believing the word of our Maker over *opinions* of sinful men. For thousands upon thousands of years, the Bible's been the only book in human history that has always proven true - and has *never* been proven false. In our Holy Book, Jesus prophesied that extreme weather, hurricanes, tsunamis, and great earthquakes would be birth pangs to usher in the "end of the age." So, the next time that you see "breaking news" headlines about historic disasters and extreme weather, are you gonna believe a liberal newscaster explaining it away as a result of climate change... or will you believe JESUS? Will you believe YHWH? Will you heed His warnings, repent of sins, and spread the word that His Son is coming back soon?

With two diametrically opposed accounts of what is causing the disasters in the world and the extreme weather, whose account are you going to trust? Will you trust the Word of our all-knowing God, or take a chance on opinions of imperfect men? Whenever severe weather strikes anywhere near my home, I find comfort in the fact that I pray to the LORD who can divert it away from my property and loved ones. I find absolutely *no* comfort whatsoever in other men telling me that the severe weather is just "random"; and that if I am "lucky," it might just pass me by. Who are *you* going to put *your* faith in? God or man? I have made my choice. Now, it is time to make yours. Choose wisely.

JESUS SAID, UPON THE EARTH (THERE SHALL BE) DISTRESS OF NATIONS, WITH PERPLEXITY; THE SEA AND THE WAVES ROARING; MEN'S HEARTS FAILING THEM FOR FEAR, AND FOR LOOKING AFTER THOSE THINGS WHICH ARE COMING ON THE EARTH: FOR THE POWERS OF HEAVEN SHALL BE SHAKEN.

- LUKE 21:25-26

CHAPTER NINE

ABORTION

BEFORE I FORMED THEE IN THE BELLY I KNEW THEE; AND
BEFORE THOU CAMEST FORTH OUT OF THE WOMB I
SANCTIFIED THEE, SAITH THE LORD.

- JEREMIAH 1:4-5

ABORTION IS MURDER... PERIOD. Human beings should not be entitled to the *choice* of murdering other humans. While many liberal women today shout "my body - my choice," they couldn't be more wrong. If the LORD has chosen to place a baby inside of your womb, then it's your responsibility to bring it into the world. God's Will always trumps your *feelings*.

There's only ever been one Woman in human history who has ever conceived outside of sexual relations, and that was the Virgin Mother of our Lord Jesus Christ. This means that virtually every single woman on this planet, who has ever become pregnant, has made a choice to bring a child into this world (with the exception of rape and forced incest). Everyone knows that sex can result in pregnancy. If you're going to sleep with someone before marriage - especially unprotected - then you're fully aware of the potential results of your actions. The day that you become pregnant with a human life inside of your womb, you should not be afforded the luxury of *choice* again. You have already made your choice, and with choices come consequences.

Now, if a teenager is not mature enough or does not have the financial means to care for a baby - or in cases of rape and incest - there are plenty of women who can and will mother the child. There are over two-million women, just in the U.S. alone, who are unable to bear children. They would gladly care for the baby. Abortion should *never* be an option. Obviously, if the life of the mother is in danger, then that's a different story - but that is a *very rare* occurrence. Dr. Landrum Shettles once said, "Less than 1% of all abortions are performed to save the mother's life." This means that 99% of abortions are *not* done to save the life of the mother. So much for that argument by abortion advocates.

As for cases of rape and incest, which are also rare, I know not allowing an abortion under such circumstances may be hard to understand and may even sound like cruel punishment to the victim; but when viewing the dilemma from a Biblical standpoint, you can see why abortion is wrong in *every instance*. In the Bible, whenever a child was conceived through rape or incest, God had always reaped out punishment for the rapists and perpetrators of incest. They never went unpunished. Also, He *never* punished the baby. He allowed babies of such horrendous crimes to live their lives. We must do the same. One victim of such tragedies should be enough. Why make two victims?! That, my friends, would be the *real* cruel punishment. The unborn baby committed no crime.

Unfortunately, there are a whole lot of abortions being done today - especially through the murderous organization known as Planned Parenthood. Their latest Annual Report revealed that the Nation's largest abortion peddler had received about $550-million from American taxpayers in the 2016-2017 fiscal year. For every adoption referral that PP had made last year, they performed over 80 abortions. They performed a total of 321,384 abortions in the most recent fiscal year. Over 300,000! That's almost 900 *per-day*.

It has been calculated that if PP were to do abortion procedures around the clock, for an entire year, they would have to abort 37 babies per-hour. That equals one dead baby *every 98 seconds* in order to reach their annual total.

Think about that... in one year, a child of God lost their life every minute and a half. What a disgrace and bloody stain on this nation. That is why it's great news to hear States are beginning to defund the abortion giant, and that over 30 Planned Parenthoods had closed their doors in 2017. Yet, the $543-million which they received from our government was a staggering 61% more than what they received a decade ago. That is one big reason why we need to defund Planned Parenthood, but I can give 7-*million* more reasons. In just 50 years, the lives of over 7-million babies have been senselessly ended by PP. Since the Supreme Court's *Roe V. Wade* ruling in 1973, legalizing abortion-on-demand nationwide, over 60-*million* babies have been murdered.

PP has been the nation's largest abortion provider since that abominable SCOTUS decision. There is no other national group that comes close. PP propagates the lie that they are a "women's health" organization that does more than abortions, but statistics tell a different story. 20 years ago, PP did over 165,000 abortions in a year. 15 years ago, they did over 230,000. 10 years ago, they cut short the lives of over 305,000 babies. Since then, they have been responsible for murdering around 320,000 infants *every year* - equaling over *3-million* murdered babies in the past 10 years.

If murdering babies was not enough to withdraw the taxpayer funding from PP (which it should be), the crooked organization has been exposed in recent years for the illegal trafficking of baby body parts - covering up child abuse and sex-trafficking - as well as promoting sex to children. Planned Parenthood is, no doubt, *of the devil*. That statement, I am sure, will draw criticism from the Americans who support the organization - but it is 100% truth.

Satan was "a murderer from the beginning" (John 8:44), and Jesus said that anyone who commits murder is a child of Satan. What Planned Parenthood is doing through abortion is ending the life of an innocent human, and murder in the Bible is defined as "shedding innocent blood." So, Biblically, PP fits the description of a "murderer" in God's Sight. Like it or not.

Something else that has long bugged me about the demonic organization is that calling themselves "Planned Parenthood" has got to be the biggest oxymoron in the entire world. How can they call themselves Planned "Parenthood," when they do everything that they possibly can to *prevent* parenthood?! PP should be sued for false advertising. They only "plan" for how mothers murder their children - never for how to raise them. Their slogan is "Care. No matter what." It should be "MURDER. No matter what."

No human being on Earth should ever be able to take the life of another human being legally. The only exceptions should be self-defense and capital punishment. If someone had committed a crime that was beyond heinous, would forever remain a threat to themselves and to others, and could not be rehabilitated, then God gives us authority to end that life. All other lives are precious in His Sight. Especially *innocent* life. And you cannot get any more innocent, or pure, than a baby who has not even exited the womb. Yet, PP is murdering over 300,000 of them every single year.

Abortion today is equivalent to false god worship of ancient times. In the Bible, we read of children being sacrificed to false gods like Baal and Molech. While children aren't being sacrificed to these or other pagan gods today, specifically, the murder of this generation's babies is just as abominable as child sacrifices of Old Testament times. The blood of innocents is being spilled, and that will warrant God's Wrath. Read verses 37 and 38 of Psalm 106 with abortion in mind, and tell me these verses don't describe our baby-killing Planned Parenthood society perfectly -

"THEY SACRIFICED THEIR SONS AND THEIR DAUGHTERS TO THE DEMONS; THEY POURED OUT INNOCENT BLOOD, THE BLOOD OF THEIR SONS AND DAUGHTERS... AND THE LAND WAS POLLUTED WITH BLOOD."

Our land today, without question, is polluted with the blood of innocents. God warns of consequences for shedding innocent blood in Exodus 23:7, Proverbs 6:17, Jeremiah 22:17, Isaiah 59:7, Matthew 18:6, Mark 9:42, and Luke 17:2. Jesus said it would be better for you to have a cinderblock tied around your neck, and to be thrown into the deepest sea, than to incur the wrath of God for harming one of His "little ones."

The number one reason why the LORD detests the crime of abortion, so very much, is because He has plans for us *before* He forms us in the womb" (Jeremiah 1:5). So, it does not matter how many days, weeks, or months, that a fetus has been forming in a woman's womb. Before it becomes a fetus, it already has *life* in God's Eyes. That is exactly why we pro-lifers defend life from the womb. We must stop arguing with unbelievers about *when* a fetus *becomes* a human, and start telling them when *God says* it does - and that is *the second* it appears in the mother's womb. If none of what I have said sways any pro-choicers from supporting Planned Parenthood, then hopefully graphic accounts of botched abortions *should* convince you.

Dr. Kermit Gosnell was an abortionist convicted of murdering at least three infants who had been "born alive" during attempted abortion procedures. In 2011, he and his employees of Women's Medical Society Clinic, in Pennsylvania, were charged with eight murder counts, 24 felonies, and 227 misdemeanors. There were seven newborns killed, when their spinal cords were severed with scissors, after being born alive. Sadly, it was not an isolated case. An undercover sting into PP exposed abortionists who had openly admitted they would "let a baby die" if a live birth were to occur in spite of an attempted abortion.

According to research by *Live Action*, and statistics that were recorded by Centers for Disease Control and Prevention (CDC), at least 500 babies are born alive following a botched abortion every year. The statistics also show that a majority of them are "left to die." What amazes me is that the same liberal activists who support Planned Parenthood are also the ones pushing for strict gun control laws to prevent mass shootings at schools. How can you say you care for the lives of America's innocent children, while at the same time, supporting an organization specializing in murdering the most innocent of them all?!

Planned Parenthood is responsible for taking *150-times more* innocent lives, each year, than mass shootings have in the past 50 years! Since the 1960s, less than 2,000 people have been killed in mass shootings. Less than 10% of victims were children or teens. 200 kids have been murdered by mass shooters in the past 50 years, while PP has murdered 320,000 babies in the previous year *alone*. If you're outraged over school shootings but also support Planned Parenthood, you are a *hypocrite* - plain and simple.

God has said that the fruit of the womb is His *"gift"* (Psalms 127:3). Sadly, many women are quick to throw His precious gifts in the trash - literally. To all of you women reading, who have had an abortion in the past but now regret the error of your ways: God wants to forgive you, but you need to do your part by repenting of your sins and asking to get washed in the sin-cleansing Blood of Jesus. He'll cleanse you not just of your sins, but of all your guilt, shame, and regret. Only then, can you live in that incomparable peace of God, which comes through forgiveness *in Christ*. Take comfort that *all* babies, everywhere, in the womb or out of it, will go to Heaven at the moment of death. While you may not have mothered your child on Earth, you will mother them someday.

On the flipside of that coin, to all women who are unrepentant after abortions, or who even shamelessly promote the abominable procedure to others: you really must be "pro-choice," because you have freely chosen Hell over Heaven for your eternal home. Heed my words while you still can... REPENT, REPENT, REPENT.

LO, CHILDREN ARE AN HERITAGE OF THE LORD: AND THE FRUIT OF THE WOMB IS HIS REWARD.

- PSALMS 127:3

CHAPTER TEN

LGBT PRIDE

WOMEN DID CHANGE THE NATURAL USE INTO THAT WHICH
IS AGAINST NATURE: AND LIKEWISE ALSO THE MEN, LEAVING
THE NATURAL USE OF THE WOMAN, BURNED IN THEIR LUST
ONE TOWARD ANOTHER; MEN WITH MEN WORKING THAT
WHICH IS UNSEEMLY, AND RECEIVING IN THEMSELVES THAT
RECOMPENCE OF THEIR ERROR WHICH WAS MEET. AND EVEN
AS THEY DID NOT LIKE TO RETAIN GOD IN THEIR
KNOWLEDGE, GOD GAVE THEM OVER TO A REPROBATE MIND,
TO DO THOSE THINGS WHICH ARE NOT CONVENIENT.

- ROMANS 1:26-28

RIGHT OFF THE BAT, so that I am not immediately condemned as being a "hateful bigot" before people even take the time to read this chapter, let me be crystal clear that I don't "hate gays." In this life, I've had close friends and colleagues who are homosexuals. Some have been as close to me as family, and I have loved them like family. So, how in the world could I possibly *hate* gays? I do not. Just as I don't hate Muslims, even though I staunchly oppose Islam. I do, however, stand against everything that is against God. Therefore, I oppose the LGBT agenda and *pride*; while I see the LGBT *people* as confused sinners who have yet to come to full knowledge of the truth.

LGBT activism, like Islam, is an anti-God religion. Yes, that's right, I called the LGBT movement a *religion*. Because, just like the Muslims or climate change activists, they hold strong beliefs which they *force* others to accept and support. That's exactly why Christianity is not a religion, but the *truth*. We don't need to force our beliefs on anyone. We simply present others with what God's Word says, and then allow them to either accept or reject it. The Godless movements that I've mentioned, on the other hand, don't afford you any such choice. For instance, with the Islamists, it is "convert or die." Climate change activists say that denial of their theory should be "criminalized." And the LGBT community says "support us - or else."

Isn't it funny how the vocal adherents to these movements all say that it is us Christians forcing our beliefs upon others? While, in reality, it is so obviously the other way around. I am not afraid to say that I stand uncompromisingly against the pride of the gay community. Pride is of Satan. Lucifer fell from Heaven because of his "pride" (Ezekiel 28). Verse 13 of Proverbs, Chapter 8, says "to fear the LORD is to hate evil; I hate *pride* and arrogance, evil behavior and perverse speech." Notice the words pride is grouped with - evil, arrogance, and perverse. Pride is not something to be celebrated, by any means.

So do I *hate* the pride, evil behavior, and perverseness of the LGBT community? You bet I do. Do I also hate the LGBT *people* themselves? Of course not. I bet you have heard it said a thousand times (and you should, because it is true) that "God hates the sin, not the sinner." He wills for all poor sinners to repent and turn to Him through His Son, Lord Jesus Christ. My friends, the Benham Brothers, say it best - "God loves all people, but He *does not* love all ideas." That is how I live my life. I love everyone, but I do not always support their actions and beliefs. I hate sin, with a passion, but I have compassion toward the people stuck in sin. I want all sinners to know that God does not approve of their behavior, but also that it is never too late to turn from their wicked ways.

For those who may not know my backstory, I wasn't always a Holy Bible thumper. A decade ago, I was the worst sinner on the block. I committed virtually every sin under the Sun, and still... *God loved me.* He pulled me out of the deep dark waters of sin, and now I try to love others as He has loved me. He gave me a new life. He gave me a second chance. I was truly *reborn* as a new creation. We all can be. We all *must be,* in order to reach His Holy Heaven. You cannot dwell in unrepentant sin, and still call yourself a Christian. You must turn and flee from sin wherever it rears its ugly head.

We ALL sin. *No one* is perfect except for Christ Jesus, and so we all fall short of God's Glory (Romans 3:23). Still, as long as you repent of sin and regret committing it, you can receive God's forgiveness and mercy every single day - through Christ. Without repentance, there can be no forgiveness... and no mercy. That is the reason I despise LGBT Pride; because there is absolutely no repentance to be found in the movement. Instead, they *celebrate* their sin - as opposed to regretting it. I wish that every Christian would view this issue through a Biblical lens; because if they did, this nation would not be in the sinful mess that it is today.

Think about it... what other sin, mentioned in God's Word, is celebrated by our society? Is blasphemy celebrated? What about dishonoring parents? Theft? Murder? Coveting? Lust? Adultery? Gossip? Lying? Drunkenness? The answer is NO to all the above. Not one of these sins is celebrated in our society, because they are recognized for what they are: SIN. Why is homosexuality treated differently from all other sins mentioned in the Holy Bible? I'm pretty sure there are far more liars, gossipers, drunkards, thieves, and adulterers in the world than homosexuals. So, why are we not celebrating any of them?

If you don't think that it is right to do so, and you believe it is inherently wrong for those sinners to be *proud* of their lifestyles, then why would you support *Gay Pride*? Why wouldn't you stand with the other sinners in their trespasses against God too? If you are going to say one sin is okay, then you might as well support them all. Otherwise, you are a *hypocrite*.

What exactly are gays so "proud" of in the first place? Has anyone ever pondered that? Are they really proud of being what God dubs "a sinner"? It sure seems like they are. They don't want to repent of their abominable lifestyle, because they see nothing wrong with it. They could care less what Almighty *God* thinks. They think that He needs to "get with the times," because they refuse to change their ways. Sodom and Gomorrah had thought the same way. How did they turn out? The Pride movement today flaunts their debaucherous sin in the same way as the inhabitants of those depraved cities of old. They have even gone so far as to take God's ancient symbol of His Covenant with mankind, the Rainbow, and make it the symbol for their rebellion against Him.

Still, there are a whole lot of Christians today who seem to have no problem standing with the LGBT movement or declaring support for their *pride*. Shame on you all. I said "a whole lot of" you because for the first time in the history of our Judeo-Christian America, a majority of Christians in this nation now *support* Gay Marriage. Nearly 60% of so-called Holy Bible "believers," to be exact, according to recent polls. Amongst all Americans, nearly 65% say that same-sex marriage should be legal, and support for homosexual relationships has climbed to 72%. God forgive us for not putting His Word first in this once-God-fearing country.

When asked whether gay sex (sodomy) was normal, 60% of Americans said they believe it is "morally acceptable - while only 37% percent said it is "morally wrong." Apparently, the morals of the USA are no longer derived from the moral Laws of Almighty God. The only thing I will ever be personally *proud* of in this life is that I'm a part of the 28% of Americans who still stand with GOD, and *against* LGBT Pride. I consider it a badge of honor to be labeled a "conservative Christian extremist." I am about as far to the Right, politically, as you can get; because I believe that is where our God is standing. Many who claim to be conservatives, who at the same time support Gay Marriage, seem to forget that we had once been dubbed the "Religious Right" for a reason.

It is because we stand firmly on and faithfully for the Word of God, without compromise. To so-called conservatives supporting Gay Marriage: you need to look up the definition of *conservative* in the dictionary. When you do, you're gonna find that you most certainly *are not one*. To fellow believers, who support the LGBT community in their pride: you, yourselves, need to repent and get right with God as much as they do! Because, when standing with them, you endorse and support their sins against the LORD. This is just as bad as committing the sins yourself. Think for a moment about who you're standing with, by meditating on Psalms 10:4 -

"IN THEIR PRIDE THE WICKED MEN DO NOT SEEK HIM; IN ALL THEIR THOUGHTS THERE IS NO ROOM FOR GOD."

Still, many of you are making *plenty of room* for "equality" in this nation today. While I agree that we're all *equally* poor sinners in God's sight, and should all be treated equally as human beings, all lifestyles and beliefs are not equal. In the adoption of a young boy, two 50-year-old men in leather chaps should not be viewed as "equal" to a Bible-based husband and wife when selecting the parents. Look, as far as homosexual relationships go, you can do whatever you want with your personal life - just as I can live my life how I choose to. God has given us all free will. So, I am not telling you how to live. I'm simply telling you how God says *not* to live! As for Gay "Marriage," I oppose it 110% - because it is an affront to the sanctity of God's Plan for mankind.

Sadly, it seems many of my brothers and sisters in the Faith have accepted that Gay Marriage is here to stay. They believe the radical LGBT agenda is too powerful to defeat. Therefore, they surrender and adopt the "if you can't beat 'em - then join 'em" mentality. My friends, the fight will never be over in the battle of good versus evil as long as we have lifebreath. As Bible believers, we cannot stand with the LGBT Pride movement *and* Almighty God. It is just not possible. You can love the sinner, but you must be very careful about getting on board with an anti-God faction. Because there is absolutely no "on the fence" with the LORD.

You cannot stand in the middle. You can't be half in and half out. You're either with Him or you're against Him. You are either in *Him* or in the *world*. Take your pick. There is right and wrong, good and evil, holy and unholy, moral and immoral, or righteous and wicked. There's absolutely no gray area with Almighty God. There never has been, and never will be. It may not be politically correct, but it is Biblically-direct, to say that the LORD is *against* the LGBT Pride movement. Does He love the people? Absolutely. He forever hopes that they will repent and turn to Him. Sadly, in their pride, the majority refuse to do so.

The Bible is dubbed by much of the homosexual community as an outdated book, with archaic laws, that needs to be revised; and liberals say that God needs to "evolve" into the 21st century. What they fail to realize is that God is *"the same yesterday, today, and forever"* (Malachi 3:6 & Hebrews 13:8). Unfortunately, even most Christians have forgotten this timeless truth. They believe Satan's lie which says that if a majority of this generation believes God is wrong on any issue, then He *must change* His stance - in order to *adapt* to the current culture. All I can say to that is don't hold your breath! God has never been, is not, and He never will be, wrong on any subject. He is GOD for God's sake!

It is us poor sinners that need to change our ways, in order to adapt to *Him*. I promise you that it is not the other way around. If the LORD called something a "sin" yesterday, then it is *still* a sin today. If He had called something an "abomination" thousands of years ago, then I assure you that it is *still* an abomination today! He is God, and so He gets to make the rules - whether this sinful generation likes it or not. There are a lot of people today who like to ignore the fact that Sodom and Gomorrah's biggest sins were homosexuality and sodomy. Yet, the U.S. Supreme Court deemed these sins perfectly normal in this nation just a few years ago.

Don't think for one second that just because this is the good ol' US of A that the LORD would treat us any differently than the rebellious nations of old. It does not matter to Him how big, rich, prosperous, or powerful a nation is. Once any nation departs from Him, He departs from them. Psalms 9:17 couldn't be more clear -

"THE WICKED SHALL BE TURNED INTO HELL, AND ALL THE NATIONS THAT FORGET GOD."

When our nation departs from its Judeo-Christian foundation, we believers must speak up. When Gay Marriage was essentially made a "law of the land" by the Godless Supreme Court in 2015, those who fear God had refused to accept that abominable ruling. #WeWillNotObey had become our battle cry across social media. Now, historically, and more so than any other group in America, Christians have always been the most obedient to the laws of this country. That is because, since the dawn of this nation, our laws have been rooted in the Law of the LORD God Almighty. But when any law of the USA comes into conflict with the laws of our God, then the national law becomes *null and void*. We can't obey. As Lord Jesus' first followers boldly proclaimed in Acts 5:29 -

"WE MUST OBEY GOD, RATHER THAN MEN."

Believers who actually support Gay Marriage would counter my Biblical take on the matter with verses from Romans 13 and Matthew 22:21. These verses of Scripture command us to obey the laws of our nation, but surely *do not apply* to unGodly laws. The laws which Lord Jesus and Paul were referring to, in the aforementioned verses, didn't come into conflict with God's Law. To any Christian using the Romans and Matthew verses to argue that the LORD would approve of His children observing unGodly laws of this world, I ask you to answer just one simple question... If the law of Rome (or any nation) ever commanded that Jews and Christians must *burn* their Torahs and Bibles, do you think Jesus and Paul would say that "You need to obey your government"?

Sorry, but I don't believe that our Lord or Saint Paul would be lighting that match. No one can read the entirety of the Bible and argue that God would ever allow us to obey worldly laws which are directly opposed to His Laws. Do you remember the Biblical prophet Daniel and what he did when he was faced with either obeying the "law of the land" or the Law of God? In Chapter 6 of Daniel, we find him living in an unGodly nation; and the King there had passed a law stating that no one but the King could offer prayers in the land. What did Daniel do? Verse 10 tells us -

"WHEN DANIEL KNEW THAT THE DECREE WAS SIGNED, HE WENT INTO HIS HOUSE; AND HIS WINDOWS BEING OPEN IN HIS CHAMBER TOWARD JERUSALEM, HE KNEELED UPON HIS KNEES THREE TIMES A DAY, AND PRAYED, AND GAVE THANKS BEFORE HIS GOD, AS HE HAD ALWAYS DONE IN THE PAST."

So, we find that Daniel "knew" of the king's law - and that he blatantly *disobeyed* it. Wow, how could a man of God ever break a national law?! It's simple... the worldly law was antithetical to God's Law. Why then is it different for us believers today? Over the past decade, America has become just as unGodly, perverted, and rebellious as Babylon. Would our God (Who was the God of

Daniel) expect us to sacrifice our Faith, in order to obey laws that violate *His* Law? I don't believe for one second that He would. I believe that He is looking for faithful Daniels in a world full of backsliders and "religious" cowards.

Putting your faith on the backburner, in order to *fit in* with the world, is extremely displeasing to the LORD. Ignoring His Word, in order to *evolve* with society, is a disgrace to Him. Violating His Commandments, in order to adhere to man's laws, is abomination in His Sight. Forgetting His Moral Law, in order to be a friend of a wicked immoral world, makes you His *enemy* (James 4:4). God has been clear that we are not to be conformed to the ways of this world in 2nd Corinthians 6:17. We know, full well, that the whole world is under the rule and influence of the devil (John 12:31 and 2nd Corinthians 4:4). That is precisely why Lord Jesus said, "The *world* hates Me, because I testify of it, that the works thereof are *evil*" (John 7:7).

Our Lord didn't mince words when teaching that we would not be accepted in a society that's hostile to the Word of God. He prophesied that true Christians, in the Last Days, would be hated - falsely accused - persecuted - imprisoned - and that our Faith would bring us into conflict with worldly rulers and laws (John 15, Mark 13, Luke 21, and Matthew 5 & 24). In our day and age, these prophecies have been (and are being) fulfilled. Since 2015's Gay Marriage ruling, so many uncompromising Bible-believers in America have been mocked - shunned - hated - sued - persecuted - attacked - and, yes, even imprisoned.

If you're a Christian or devout Jew that isn't being labeled a hater, bigoted, discriminatory, or a Bible-thumping looney-tune regarding your stances on hot button social issues of our day, then you're not reading God's Word right. *Read it again.* If you have read it, front to back, you're probably cherry-picking parts of the Bible that suit *your* worldview - not God's. You cannot pick and choose what you want to believe, and discard the rest. You cannot render some of God's Word untrue, simply because you disagree with it. The Word of the LORD is not going to be popular in this evil, perverted, and rebellious generation. You can't expect to be loved by all, holding a Biblical worldview. Turn on your TV, and you'll see God's Word mocked and blasphemed without remorse.

Along with not believing all of the Bible, there are Christians who use Biblical verses out of context in order to justify support for the LGBT agenda. Verses like, "We all sin and fall short of the Glory of God" or "Judge not" are widely used to defend same-sex relationships. I'd like to counter those arguments once and for all. As I stated earlier, it's 100% true that we "*all sin*"; but that is also why we *all need* Jesus. That's why God calls us *all* to repentance. Is the gay community repenting? Are they kneeling at the Cross of Christ, acknowledging their need for Him? If they have been, I must've missed it. The fact is that they have not repented, because they don't believe they are sinners. So, while we *all* sin, sadly, we do not *all* repent.

As to the "judge not" verse, which unbelievers all across the world have memorized to justify just about every sin in the Book, have you read the verse, "Show my people *their sins*"? Making someone aware that they are sinning is *not* judging. What Lord Jesus meant (in context) was for us to not go around being critical of someone else's sins, while we ourselves are laden with them. I, myself, repent daily; because I acknowledge that I sin every day, whether I realize it or not. If I were to walk around claiming to be "holier than thou," while condemning the sins of everyone else, *then* I would be judging. To make someone (who does not know God) aware that their lifestyle is against His Word is not judging them, but rather *loving* them.

I do not want to see anyone end up in Hell at the end of the road. Apparently, the "judge not" Christians will have no problem watching them burn. When believers err on the side of political correctness, refusing to condemn celebration of LGBT lifestyles, we push confused souls further into Satan's hands. We are called to be the light in this dark world, and God expects us to be the moral compass. If we aren't being either of these things, then we may be judged by God as harshly as unrepentant sinners. For the LORD is not willing that any perish, but that *all* would come to repentance (2nd Peter 3:8).

If you are telling the gay community that they are "all good," have nothing to worry about, and that God loves them "just the way they are," they will not come to repentance - and will perish in Hell. God isn't willing that they should, but apparently you are just fine with it. The demonic forces that are possessing the gay community can only be cast out and defeated by the sinless Blood of the Lamb of God, Christ *JESUS*. The homosexuals will never approach the Saviour of the world if they don't believe that there is anything they need to be *saved from*. They will never repent if Christians don't have the cojones to tell them that they are wrong. So, do not be afraid to speak up and show them their sins! Their eternal lives very well may depend on it.

I can't finish this chapter without addressing the Transgender insanity that is sweeping across our nation and the world. Call me old-fashioned, but I still see things the way that God created them to be. When I was growing up in the 80's and 90's, boys still liked girls and girls still liked boys. Boys were still boys and girls were still girls. Today, you never know what someone is half the time. People are calling themselves transgender, pangender, cisgender, gender-fluid, genderqueer, even *genderless*. It's utterly ridiculous.

Modern society has been making war (virtually unopposed by the Church) on every single truth of God's Word - I mean *every* truth - such as the most basic truth of all, that "In the Beginning, God created them *male* and *female*." This verse is plain and to the point. There should be no wiggle room for other interpretations. God made man, and then God made woman. He said to be fruitful and multiply, and so they had sexual relations and made babies.

That is the reason why all of us are here today! If Adam decided one day that he wanted to be the woman, or Eve decided that she wore the pants in the garden, there would've never been an Abel, Seth, Enoch, Noah, Shem, Abraham, Isaac, Jacob (Israel), Judah, Joseph, Moses, David, Elijah, Daniel, nor our Lord Jesus Christ.

The human race would have died out 6,000 years ago if they thought like today's society. Since the dawn of Earth, as we know it, there have been only two genders - male and female. Period. First, God had created man, and then He created woman *for* man. If God thought that it was okay for Adam to lay with other men, then God would have created another man. He didn't. He created Eve. The LORD also calls for a union of marriage - for a husband to take a wife, and for them to cleave together and become "one flesh." He created men and women with their distinct body parts that come together to produce offspring. You cannot produce kids with two male parts or two female parts. Basic human biology!

In 2012, the American Psychiatric Association had referred to "gender identity disorder" as a mental health problem. In the eyes of God, it most certainly is. While society tells you to encourage your kids to find their own *identity*, Almighty God already gave them one at birth. The Book of Proverbs, Chapter 22 and verse 6, commands us to "Train up a child in the way they should go; and when they are old, they will not depart from it." Christian parents must be more active in the lives of their children than ever before; because if you're not raising them, be sure that someone else *will*.

I personally could care less if a man or woman gets offended when I call them what God created them to be, which is a *man* or a *woman*. If their feelings are hurt because I don't refer to them by another pronoun, then they should take it up with their Creator - not me. His language was not vague when He said that men and women shouldn't live in a fantasyland, nor play make-believe, by dressing up like the opposite sex. In Deuteronomy 22:5, He said...

"THE WOMAN SHALL NOT WEAR THAT WHICH PERTAINETH UNTO A MAN, NEITHER SHALL A MAN PUT ON A WOMAN'S GARMENT: FOR ALL THAT DO SO ARE ABOMINATION UNTO THE LORD THY GOD."

ABOMINATION. Get it?! We believers cannot tiptoe around Biblical truth, in order to not offend somebody. I do not care how many sex changes someone like Bruce Jenner has had or will ever have. He can call himself "Caitlyn" all day long, but he'll always be Bruce *the man* to me. That is what he will forever be in God's Sight. It has gotten so bad today that we're actually debating over Transgender Bathroom Bills to decide whether or not grown men should be allowed in the same restroom as little girls. Craziness! There should be no debate. If you were born with male parts, then you use the men's room. If you were born with female parts, then you use the ladies' room. Period. End of story!

God-fearing people in this nation and world need to stand up and say ENOUGH IS ENOUGH. If we don't speak out against this insanity, then who else will? It is high time for us believers to be the desperately needed adults in the room.

THOU SHALT NOT LIE WITH MANKIND, AS WITH WOMANKIND: IT IS ABOMINATION.

- LEVITICUS 18:22

CHAPTER ELEVEN

FALLING AWAY FROM THE FAITH

NOW THE SPIRIT SPEAKETH EXPRESSLY, THAT IN THE LATTER
TIMES SOME SHALL DEPART FROM THE FAITH, GIVING HEED
TO SEDUCING SPIRITS, AND DOCTRINES OF DEVILS.

- 1ST TIMOTHY 4:1

JUST OVER A DECADE ago, in 2007, there were approximately 227-million adults in the United States. Nearly 80% of them had identified as Christian. Between 2007 and 2014, while the overall size of this country's population grew by about 20-million, those who identified as Christians shrunk to around 70% - about a 10% decline, and a net decline of roughly 5-million.

Today, 70% of millennials (aged 18-33) believe Christianity is alienating young adults by being too "judgmental" about LGBT issues. 31% of them, who've been raised in Christian households, say they're now unbelievers because of negative Biblical teaching about gay and lesbian people. Half (45%) of young Evangelicals (aged 18-29) actually *support* Gay Marriage. They are professing Christians, mind you, not unbelievers. While they may profess the Faith, and are churchgoers, they are obviously not being reared in Godly homes. If they were, then their parents would instruct them in the Biblical truth and teach them to fear God. If nearly half of this generation's young Evangelicals endorse same-sex Marriage, then their parents should be ashamed.

Recent statistics have revealed that nearly 7 in 10 American seniors (67%) are Christians, while less than 3 in 10 (29%) are young adults. Evangelicals had made up 22% of the population in 1988. 20 years later, they remained strong at 21% (in 2008). As of 2015, that number rapidly dropped to 17%. This means there was only a 1% drop in two decades, and nearly a 5% drop in just a 7-year period! While there are many reasons for the massive falling away from the Faith which we've seen in America (and the world at large) throughout the past decade, the number one reason was former President Obama's radical transformation of America.

During his tenure, the United States devolved into a cesspool of Biblically-hostile attitudes and beliefs. Islam was celebrated, while Christianity was targeted as "hateful" and "bigoted." Israel was treated like an enemy, as opposed to our greatest Ally. The schools forced the Godless theories of evolution, Big Bang, and climate change on America's youth. Our culture was flooded with blasphemy, violence, sex, legalization of mind-altering drugs, and LGBT propaganda. Add the cowardly backslidden Church to the mix, and we had a recipe for disaster. Worldly pastors were afraid (and most still are) to preach Biblical truth. They were afraid of losing liberal congregants in their pews, being targeted by Obama for discrimination or threatened by Islamists and LGBT bullies.

Too many churches in our once-God-fearing Nation did not, and will not, even preach on *sin*. The reason we are supposed to come to Jesus and go to church, in the first place, is because we are all poor sinners! Once you stop teaching what sin is, why we must repent of it, and why we need a Saviour because of it, there would be no need for Christianity. Unfortunately, our Faith today is not about Lord Jesus dying on the Cross to reconcile the sinful world to the Father. Instead, it's become about entertainment, and "feel good" time for so-called believers.

Honestly, you don't even need to be a Holy Bible believer to attend church these days. You are more likely to see a secularized concert, a few skits, and hear a poem from the pastor, as opposed to getting taught God's Word. This is primarily because, in the early 2000's, Rick Warren (who is wrongly dubbed "America's Pastor") influenced Christian leaders across the United States to join his blasphemous *"Purpose Driven Church"* movement. The sinner-friendly plan for churches that Warren laid out, in order to gain larger audiences and appeal to unbelievers, set forth a list of do's and don'ts for pastors.

Some of the most troubling suggestions that Warren laid out were: *don't* mention sin - *don't* say "saved" or "unsaved," but use the words "churched" and "unchurched" instead - *don't* mention Hell - *don't* give altar calls to "accept Jesus as Saviour" - *remodel* churches to resemble venues like nightclubs or casinos, in order to be more inviting to sinners - allow coffee and snacks in pews with no dress code - and have hip music (such as hard rock, hip hop, or heavy metal) to attract the youth. I am sure that every one of you has a church doing one (or all) of these things in your local area, as we speak.

Though I disagree with all of the above, the two that hurt the Church the most are not preaching on sin or Hell. If there is NO sin, then where's the need for *the Saviour*? If NO Hell, then what are any of us trying to live good lives for in the first place? If we are all going to Heaven, then we might as well just *live it up*. Any pastors today not preaching on either one of these all-important Biblical issues will be guilty of their flocks ending up in the Hell they conveniently fail to mention. At least church memberships will continue to grow in the meantime! It's sickening. This is one of the biggest reasons why our society is laden with sin more so than ever before.

Christian "leaders" today who have been given a charge by God to "cry aloud, and spare not to show the people their *sins*"

(Isaiah 58:1), are doing the exact opposite. They are saying that sin is OK, because "we all do it, so why judge"? They ignore the reality that, from the beginning, sin *kills*. Saint Paul said that "the wages of sin is death" (Romans 6:23); and for the disease of sin there is but *one* remedy: God's Only Begotten Son, JESUS. If today's churches are not teaching this central truth of our Faith, then it really doesn't matter how many "Christians" are sitting in our houses of worship. None of them are getting saved, and they are going to be unpleasantly surprised when they don't meet God at the end of the road.

Also, because of not being taught Biblical truth in churches today, more and more believers are embracing false doctrines like the Big Bang theory, evolution, and Replacement Theology. Some "Christians" no longer accept that Jesus Christ is the *Only Way* to Heaven, though God's Word emphatically states that *He is* around 1,000 times. If they were actually being taught the Bible in their churches, they'd know that. Instead, it has become acceptable in Christian circles to say that Muslims, Buddhists, Hindus, witches, and other false god worshippers are going to the "same Heaven" that we are in the end. That statement may be politically correct, but it is 100% Biblically incorrect.

A 2017 survey found only 25% of American Christians feel that they have a personal responsibility to share the Gospel with others, and only 40% believe that the Holy Bible is truly the *Word of God*. If this were just a study of all Americans, it'd be sad but not surprising. The fact only professing Christians participated in the survey is extremely alarming. How can anyone call themself Christian, and say they have no obligation to preach the Gospel to others? Are we reading the same Bible?! Are we worshipping the same Jesus Christ? The Jesus who'd said, "Go into all the world and proclaim the Gospel to the *whole creation*" (Mark 16:15 and Matthew 28:19-20)?

What is worse than believers not sharing the Gospel message is that the study also revealed that only 1 in 4 pastors say they feel a responsibility to share it. Apparently, Warren's "purpose driven" pastors are still thriving. It seems their only purpose is to fill seats and sell self-help books. They're focusing on being friends of *the world*, rather than desiring to hear "well done, good and faithful servant" from our Lord in Heaven someday. It is no wonder this generation's Christians are Biblically ignorant! Even their pastors don't truly know the Word of God.

I can understand some Christians not being able to recite the Ten Commandments, not being able to name a few of the 16 Old Testament prophets, or even not being able to explain the Trinity or the Rapture. What I cannot possibly begin to grasp is how 3/4 of American believers and pastors don't understand that the basic preaching of the Gospel to the lost is the *heart* of Christianity. If they don't believe in evangelizing others, then I believe that they are in the wrong Faith. Christianity is all about taking the "Good News" of what Jesus Christ did for us at Calvary, and sharing it with everyone we can in this life. Jesus taught this so many times. There is no way you could miss it if you are a true believer.

Read the "Parable of the talents," or when Jesus taught of not hiding a lamp under a bushel, or when He said the Gospel must be preached to *all nations* before He'd return. Our Lord couldn't have stressed strongly enough that we are not to keep salvation to ourselves. We've been called to share the message of God's Grace with the entire world. I love the saying, "we are not saved to be silent." It's so very true. It's so very Biblical. Too many Christians today want to accept the Gift of God, but then selfishly keep it all to themselves - keeping the Gospel message confined to their own homes or to their church.

Sharing the Gospel with others is one of the primary duties of a Christian in this life. The only two duties that ever come before it are repentance of sins, and acceptance of Jesus as our personal

Lord and Saviour. So, since 75% of Christians today don't believe in sharing the Gospel, I am sure that most American believers do not even know what it is. It is simple, and Saint Paul laid it out in detail in 1st Corinthians, Chapter 15 and verses 1-4 –

"I DECLARE UNTO YOU THE GOSPEL WHICH I PREACHED UNTO YOU, WHICH YOU HAVE RECEIVED... HOW THAT CHRIST DIED FOR OUR SINS ACCORDING TO THE SCRIPTURES; AND THAT HE WAS BURIED, AND THAT HE ROSE AGAIN THE THIRD DAY ACCORDING TO THE SCRIPTURES."

If you don't want to share this message with others, then you are no Christian at all. You need to truly *get saved*, because you quite obviously are not. I don't mean to come across being harsh with fellow believers, but I don't think you can call yourself a true believer if you don't feel the need to bring others to Christ.

Nearly 20% of Christians (not unbelievers) today believe that "men" wrote the Holy Bible - not the Holy Spirit of God. Only 40% of American Christians say that the Bible is the Word of Almighty God. What a disgrace. Also, 37% of Christians say that reading the Bible is "*not essential*" to being a believer. So, the Book which led you to become a Christian, in the first place, is no longer important once you officially *are one*? Ridiculous! Today's wishy washy, don't offend anyone, PC, unBiblical Christianity is a big reason why America's been cursed for decades. Christians not doing their job of preaching our God's Word to the heathen is leading the rest of this nation straight to Hell in a handbasket.

Instead of preaching the truth to their congregations, churches are *rewriting it*. The dangerous confusion of the "Gender-fluid" movement, which has been sweeping the world, is spreading into Christianity. As far-fetched as it sounds, prepare to be shocked as to just how much this fallacy has been embraced in mainstream Christian institutions and churches across the world.

There are many churches today, like the Church of Sweden and Episcopal Church of Washington, DC, who urge their clergy to stop referring to the LORD as "Male." Though all of the Books in Jewish and Christian Scriptures leave no doubt that He is, some churches have decided they no longer want to worship the God of the Holy Bible. They would rather cower to the demands of our backslidden society, reinvent our God, and sacrifice eternal truth, in order to appease sinners with a politically correct delusion. The Bible never minces words about God being Male.

1st Corinthians, Chapter 8 and verse 6, states, "There is but One God, the *Father*, from whom all things came and for whom we live; and there is but One Lord, Jesus Christ, through whom all things came and through whom we live." All throughout the entirety of both Old and New Testaments, YHWH God is referred to as our Father in Heaven and as "He" or "Him." And Lord Jesus wasn't some made up character in a fable or fairytale. Historical records outside of the Bible prove HE was a real, living, breathing *Man* on Earth. How could any believer, or entire denominations composed of theologians, ever approve of publicly denying these facts? Worse, how could they approve of replacing the facts with something that they know darn well to be a flat-out LIE?

Many backslidden churches today are using "Gender-neutral" language to replace instances of "Lord - He - His - Him" in their services. Some will not even utter the Names of YHWH, Jesus Christ, or the Holy Spirit any longer - diverting simply to using the generic word "God." Also, "The Father, the Son, and the Holy Spirit" is replaced in churches with "God and the Holy Trinity." This destroys the Doctrine that the Christian Church is supposed to be teaching the world. How can they say God "*and*" the Holy Trinity? The Father, the Son, and the Holy Spirit ARE God. The new language used implies that there is *another* God besides the Holy Trinity. This is blasphemy and heresy.

Modern churches are filled with false prophets today. Christ Jesus prophesied one of the signs of His return would be a world full of false prophets and "wolves in sheep's clothing" (Matthew 7 & 24). He said they'd deceive and lead believers astray in the Last Days, and countless believers have no doubt been led astray with this gender-neutral nonsense! It has even found its way into popular translations of the Bible. In 2016, SBC (Southern Baptist Convention) published their Christian Standard Bible (CSB); and to the surprise of many, a number of the gender-neutral elements which the SBC long condemned were inserted into its translation.

The CSB translated "anthropos," a Greek word for "man," in gender-neutral form over 150 times - rendering it as "human" or "people" instead. Concerning Jesus' incarnation, the "likeness of men" becomes "likeness of humanity." Also, "Adelphoi" (Greek for "brother") appears in gender-neutral form 100+ times. "Men" had been replaced with "humans, humanity, humankind, people, or persons" about 250 times. There were many other instances of gender-neutral replacements for masculine terminology found all throughout CSB. YHWH warned in Deuteronomy 4:2, and Jesus repeated the warning in the Book of Revelation (22:18-19), that there is severe eternal punishment that awaits anyone adding to or taking away from the words of the Holy Bible.

Unfortunately, there's so much of this occurring all across our world; and the gender-neutral craze has been playing a huge role in it. Whether done through ignorance, or with full knowledge of breaking the LORD's commands, every guilty party has to repent. Some are deceived by Satan to think by being more inclusive they are leading more people to God. On the contrary, by ignoring or rewriting key verses of the Bible, and hiding the truth of God to avoid offending someone, they lead their converts straight to Hell.

There are even mainline Christian denominations today who are turning their backs on God's beloved Nation of Israel. There is no nation that is mentioned more within the pages of our Holy

Bibles; and the LORD could not be any more clear, in the Holiest Book on Planet Earth, that He is forever the "God of Israel." Still, Presbyterians, Methodists, Episcopalians, and others, have joined the anti-Israel BDS movement - which calls for the destruction of the Jewish State. What Bible are these denominations reading? It is certainly not my version, nor any legitimate version that I am familiar with for that matter.

On top of all this, for the first time in our Judeo-Christian Nation's history, a majority of Christians support Gay Marriage - 55% of so-called Bible believers, according to the recent polling. Many churches now perform same-sex marriage ceremonies, and even ordain homosexual or transgender priests and pastors. Some have even held "Gay Pride" events inside of their church! Along with the Methodist Church, United Church of Christ, Presbyterian Church USA, and the Episcopal Church, about 30 denominations now endorse the LGBT agenda. These are supposed to be Houses of God, but they have now shamefully become dens of sin!

Finally, no chapter about backslidden churches and Christian leaders would be complete without mention of uber-liberal Pope Francis. The current Pope of the Roman Catholic Church has told his flock that "the Quran, and the spiritual teachings contained in it, is just as valid as the Holy Bible." NO. It most certainly is not. It is a book that is filled with brutality, cruelty, ruthlessness, and bloodshed; while our Book's a Love Story between God and man. It's filled with grace, forgiveness, mercy, and peace. How can the Pope, who is so ignorant to the polar opposites of Christianity and Islam, be the leader of billions of Christians globally?!

In 2015, Francis was the first Pope, in all of world history, to hold Islamic prayers in Vatican square and to allow reading of the Quran in church services. If this Pope really believed the Bible, then he would acknowledge that the teachings of Islam's Quran are antithetical to our Holy Book's teachings. The Quran denies that Jesus is the Christ and the Son of God; and it teaches that

Muhammad, the warmonger pedophile false prophet of Islam, is "greater than Jesus." The Quran says Jesus returns "as a Muslim," destroys every Cross, and murders every Christian and Jew who does not convert to Islam. On top of that, Islam's "messiah" (the Mahdi) is said to do everything the Antichrist is prophesied to do! Our sacred Books, and our Gods, are *most definitely not the same.*

There have also been some other red flags raised about the Pope's sincerity to Biblical doctrine, such as his stance toward the Nation of Israel. Since assuming power, Francis has been much more of a friend to Israel's terrorist neighbors in Palestine than he has been to our God's Nation. And, if all of this was not troubling enough, the Pope has spoken out in favor of evolution and the Big Bang. He has said, "When we read about Creation in Genesis, we run the risk of imagining God was a magician, with a magic wand able to do everything, but that is not so." Wow. The blasphemous words that you just read were not spoken by atheist Bill Maher, nor by Creation-mocker Bill Nye, but by a man who is revered by so many - the world over - as the "mouthpiece of God."

He has also said that "Evolution in nature is not inconsistent with the notion of Creation." Evolution is *completely* inconsistent with the Creation account. God says that He created man in *His Image*, not in the image of a monkey! Christian belief in evolution is a slap in the Face of Almighty God, and is nothing but a bunch of monkey-business. This "progressive" Pope has even urged the Vatican's Bishops to ease the language on same-sex unions, and has said that atheists will get to Heaven by their "good deeds." Our Holy Bible says that we are "not saved" by any of "our own deeds," but by Faith in Christ *alone.*

I truly believe that Francis could be the "False Prophet" of the Last Days, whom we read about in Revelation (Chapter 13). That leader, who rises to power in the season of the Antichrist, will be a globally-influential Christian leader. He'll visibly represent the Church on Earth, but through words and deeds he will destroy it.

He also ushers in a One-World-Religion; and given Pope Francis' ignorant comments on Islam, this appears to be something that he would be in favor of. Many of you may not be aware that when Francis (Jorge Bergoglio) had been announced as the new Pope on global television, the exact time was 7:06 pm (Rome time) - 66 minutes past 6:00 pm, or 6:66! Just something for my Catholic family and friends to ponder.

Please understand that this is not an attack on all Catholics. I have family members and friends who are. I am just warning you all to not be led astray by the current leader of the global Church of Rome. I suspect he will be responsible for numerous Christians *falling away* from the Faith, so do not be deceived! There are too many believers who are. There are also too many self-proclaimed Christians today who "know of" Jesus Christ, but have never truly "known" Him. As someone who has walked with Jesus, for over a decade, I don't think you can walk away from Him after enjoying a personal relationship with Him. Christians who have departed, are departing, or will depart, from the Faith - turning their backs on Christ - were *never* truly saved in the first place. End of story.

LET NO MAN DECEIVE YOU BY ANY MEANS: FOR THAT DAY (OF CHRIST'S COMING) SHALL NOT COME, EXCEPT THERE COME A FALLING AWAY FIRST, AND THAT MAN OF SIN BE REVEALED, THE SON OF PERDITION.

- 2ND THESSALONIANS 2:3

CHAPTER TWELVE

FAITHLESS GENERATION

JESUS SAID, O FAITHLESS AND PERVERSE GENERATION, HOW
LONG SHALL I BE WITH YOU? HOW LONG SHALL I SUFFER
(PUT UP WITH) YOU?

- MATTHEW 17:17/MARK 9:19/LUKE 9:41

A 2017 STUDY BY the Barna Group discovered that Generation
Z is the "*least Christian Generation*" in American history. Gen-Z
is made up of those born between the years 1999-2015. It is very
fitting that the generation is labeled "Z," since the letter signifies
the end. After reading the past eleven chapters, I think someone
would have a hard time arguing that we are not living in the End
Times described in the Holy Bible. I also find it interesting that
the current generation of teenagers began in 1999, which happens
to be three upside down sixes. The infamous 6-6-6 of Revelation
13:18 is associated with the "Mark of the Beast" (the Antichrist).

To be perfectly clear, I am not saying that every child born in
'99 is a child of the devil. There are plenty of fine young people
that are actually being raised right in this generation. I'm also not
saying that the entire generation is "of Satan." What I am saying,
which is backed up by the recent Barna Study, is that Generation
Z is more prone to following after him than any other generation
in our nation's history. The Bible prophesies that a majority of the

"Last Days" generation will worship Antichrist (i.e. Satan), and the LORD says that there will be a great falling away from His Word during this perverse, faithless, and demonically-influenced final generation. You'd be hard-pressed to argue those adjectives do not apply perfectly to the society in which we live.

In the "Generation Z Research Project," Barna conducted a total of four focus groups with U.S. teenagers between the ages of 14 and 17, and had also conducted two national surveys. The first survey, conducted in November of 2016, interviewed about 1,500 teens aged 13 to 18. The second survey was conducted in July of 2017, and interviewed just over 500 teens of the same age group. Barna's research had revealed that only 4 out of 100 teens hold a Biblical worldview. 4%! That is scary. Also, more teens than ever before identify as atheists. The study indicated that 35% of teens consider themselves atheist, agnostic, or not religiously affiliated. That is close to *half* of the generation!

Barna's findings also showed that almost twice as many teens in Gen-Z claimed to be atheists than Millennials: 13% compared to 7%, and less than 60% of Gen-Z teens consider themselves as Christian - compared to 65% of Millennials, and 75% of the Baby Boomers. While you would think that it is a small positive (in a research study full of negatives) that nearly 6 in 10 Gen-Z teens identified as Christians, remember that only 4% of them actually hold the Biblical worldview. They most likely only check off the religion box as Christians because that is what their parents are, but they themselves do not live or believe the Faith which they claim to be a part of. Sadly, Barna's study had exposed a lack of Biblical faith among all age groups in America today.

Using a classification of Faith based on the widely accepted orthodox Christian beliefs, Barna developed a set of theological criteria that each respondent had to meet in order to be classified as holding the Biblical worldview. The percentage of Americans whose beliefs qualified them for the worldview declines in each successively younger generation: 10% of Baby Boomers, 7% of Gen-X, and 6% of Millennials, see the world through a Biblical lens - compared to only 4% of Gen-Z.

The research also found that only about 60% of "churched teens" had agreed that the Bible is "totally accurate" in all of the principles that it teaches. This means that nearly 1/2 of American teens, being raised in Christian homes, do not believe what they are being taught. I suspect much of that has to do with the utter lack of Biblical faith among their peers. When a majority of their friends and this generation mock God, it must be very difficult for young impressionable minds to stay true to Him. As I said at the start of this chapter, the devil wants to claim this generation as his own; and, unfortunately, he appears to be succeeding.

After nearly a decade of false religions being pushed into our country (while the true God was forced out), national embrace of homosexuality and transgenderism, and the demonic mainstream media forcing sex - violence - drugs - and Godless music down the throats of the youth on a daily basis, it is no wonder Gen-Z doesn't want to know the God with a *moral* Law. Satan is loving every minute of it. He's the author of confusion after all.

One big thing that the devil has succeeded in confusing this young generation about is their gender. Instead of saying "I was born a boy, so I'm a boy," like every other generation in history, Satan has so many lost souls thinking they are *anything but* what they entered into this world as. Barna found that 12% of Gen-Z identified sexually as something other than heterosexual, with 7% saying they are "bisexual." These are just *kids,* mind you! Barna's President, David Kinnaman, said this was "the highest percentage of self-identified non-heterosexuals ever seen in *any* generation."

Sadly, it is not just the middle and high school crowd that the devil has been confusing, deceiving, and manipulating. He is also infiltrating this country's colleges through atheist professors who mock God, belittle the Bible, and teach the Big Bang, evolution, and climate change as unquestionable truth. All of these theories are designed to pull us away from faith in our Creator, and they appear to be succeeding with a large portion of our population.

A 2016 *LifeWay* study revealed that over 50% of Americans rarely or *never* read the Holy Bible, and that only 1 in 10 hold a Biblical worldview. 25% of 18-24 year olds in America admitted that they have *never* read the Bible at all. No, haven't even picked it up off of the shelf. Only a minuscule 2% of this age group said they've read "most of the Bible." 2 percent! God help us. 52% of Americans believe that the Holy Bible is simply a "good source of morals," 37% feel it's just "helpful," only 36% believe it to be "true," 34% call it just "a story," and 14% say that it is "outdated." That all sure explains a lot about why this nation has been in such a sad state, and seems to only be getting worse year after year.

This isn't just happening in America either, as there are other historically-Christian nations that are falling away from the Faith as well. In 2017, it was reported that the Church of England is facing a catastrophic fall in the proportion of young adults who describe themselves as Christian. Data shows a rapid acceleration toward a secular society. For the first time in history, more than half of the population of the United Kingdom say that they have "no religion"; and only 8% of UK adults (under age 24) describe themselves as a form of Christian, while a whopping 75% of their 18-24 year-olds say that they have "no Faith at all."

I believe that much of the decline in Biblical belief has had to do with the influence of God-hating mainstream media. Whether it be television, movies, music, the internet, or dirtrag newspapers and magazines, people are inundated with demonic messaging - perversion - celebration of sin - and blatant blasphemy. A popular men's magazine, *GQ*, made headlines in 2018, when its writers placed the Bible on a list of "*21 Books You Don't Have to Read.*" That sure puts *GQ* at the top of the list for magazines a Christian or Jew should never read!

The editors of the magazine all chose their own books for the list, writing in the introduction - "We have been told all our lives that we can only call ourselves well-read once we have read the Great Books. We tried... We realized that not all the Great Books have aged well. Some are racist and some are sexist, but most are just really, really boring." Writer Jesse Ball was the ignoramus who added the Holy Bible to the list. He wrote that the Bible is "foolish, repetitive, and contradictory," and also said, "the Bible is rated very highly by all the people who supposedly live by it, but who in actuality have not read it... Those who have read it know there are some good parts, but overall it is certainly not the finest thing that man has ever produced."

He is right in one tiny aspect of his inaccurate criticism, and that is when he said it was "not the finest thing that *man* has ever produced." He is right, because "man" didn't write the Holy Bible - *God did*. So, it truly is the finest thing ever produced on Planet Earth - by GOD. Holy men of God penned the Bible through the inspiration of His Holy Spirit (2nd Peter 1:21). Had Ball actually read the Holiest Book on Earth, then he'd know that. For those unfamiliar with him (as I was), Ball apparently penned around 15 books. How many of them have you heard of? As for me, *not one*. I am sure you all can say the same.

I guess it is some kind of inferiority complex that Ball and other critics of the Bible struggle with. As a failing author, he has to resort to attacking the greatest Author of all-time in order to garner some attention. He did accomplish the goal of getting his otherwise unheard-of name out there. Heck, I had to take the time to mention him in this book. At what cost did he make his name known though? His attack on the Holy Bible garnered far more negative press than positive, and he unfortunately sold his soul for 15 minutes of fame (more like 15 seconds). Sadly, we live in an age where the lamestream media pushes boundaries to gain more followers; and not even blasphemy is out of bounds today.

Ball, and many other critics of God's Word love to argue that there are errors and contradictions. Though, they can never point out even one solid example. I have personally read the Holy Bible front-to-back at least seven times, throughout the past decade, and I've never found one error nor contradiction. If God's Word really was "foolish" and "contradictory," like Ball claims, how is it the Best-selling Book of *all-time* - selling at least 100-million copies annually? I am curious as to how many copies of Ball's books, or *GQ*, have been sold? Yet, they seem to think they know what is better for the world than the LORD does. It is the blasphemous content, which they and a majority of the media promote, that is turning some people downright demonic these days.

It's one thing to not believe in God, but there are far too many atheists who flat-out hate Him and His Word with a passion. At a Louisiana Town Hall in 2017, hosted by Republican Senator Bill Cassidy, a group of raucous Democrat protesters had erupted in anger during the opening Prayer. The second that the Chaplain, Michael Sprague, announced that he would open the event with a Prayer, the crowd became unruly and began shouting him down. Childish hecklers yelled "Prayer?! Pray on your own time. This is our time!" and "Separation of Church and State!" Not even a few seconds into the prayer, one attendee had rudely shouted, "Amen! We're done. Shut up!" A woman shouted "Lucifer" (the original name of Satan) when the Chaplain mentioned God.

When he closed the prayer "in the Name of Jesus," the room of rowdy Democrats had erupted in riotous anger and booed him. Immediately following the Town Hall, Cassidy said to reporters, "Wow, they booed the Name of *Jesus*." And Sprague said, "I have never been shouted down throughout a time of Prayer like that. I've never been in a situation like that. It's sad there wasn't honor and respect for God." It is beyond sad, disgusting, and alarming that human beings like this exist in our once-God-fearing nation.

Though shocking, on so many levels, this wasn't the first time the Democrats were publicly enraged at the mere mention of God.

During the 2012 Election, while drafting the Party's platform for Obama's second term, the Democrat leaders had removed *all* references to GOD - along with any pro-Israel language. They did not ignorantly forget to mention God either. The leaders came to the conscious decision to *remove Him*. When the absence of God in the platform was discovered, it became headline news. Dems realized that they would need to put God back into the picture, or else risk losing Christian votes for Obama. So, an amendment to the platform was placed on the Democratic Convention agenda. The amendment would serve to restore the mention of God to the platform, but the Dems would find that it wouldn't be an easy fix.

The Democrat Party, under 4 years of Obama, had moved so far away from God that the delegates of their Convention actually opposed the amendment and loudly *booed* the restoration of God into the platform. Besides booing or shouting down the Names of Jesus or God, there are also many Democrat politicians who want absolutely nothing to do with the LORD. The former president, Barack Hussein Obama, put our Heavenly Father and Lord on the backburner for eight long years. At the same time, he uplifted the god of Islam and other false gods of foreign religions.

At a Georgetown University Speech, in 2009, Obama ordered the Name of Jesus to be covered up with a black drape while he spoke there. He had also deliberately omitted the word "Creator" many times when quoting the Declaration of Independence in his public speeches. Obama's administration made numerous public apologies for Qurans being burned by the U.S. military in 2012. Though, when it was revealed that our military burned Bibles in the Middle East, his administration gave several reasons why it was "the right thing to do." I could go on and on about how he publicly mocked the Holy Bible, and disrespected our God, but that would be a whole 'nother book in itself.

I believe the Biblically-hostile 44th President, and the popular liberal celebrities of our day, have emboldened God-haters to take blasphemy to alarming new heights in this country. During the 2017 International Women's Day March, abortion advocates had carried placards depicting Mary (the Virgin Mother of our Lord Jesus) as a bloody vagina. One disgusting sign read, "If Mary had an abortion we wouldn't be in this mess." The *Huffington Post* has published many blasphemous articles over the years, but a piece by Suzanne Dewitt Hall may have taken the cake as the worst yet. She penned an article claiming that Mary was "transgender," and that Jesus was the "first transgender man." Un-freakin-believable!

20 years ago, blasphemous content like that would have been blacklisted, the writer would be shamed, and publications printing such garbage would end up in the trash bin of history where they belong. Sadly, in today's day and age, that kind of filth is not only acceptable, but it's become commonplace in our society. Things have gotten so bad in this country that Nativity scenes and Ten Commandments statues at State Capitols have been taken down, and replaced with Satanic monuments! No joke. After complaints from atheists about Christianity and Judaism taking precedence over other faiths on government property (which they absolutely should, given our national history), states like Oklahoma, Florida, and Michigan displayed Satanic monuments on Capitol lawns.

On top of that, something that would have been unheard of a decade ago, places of Satanic worship are springing up all across this country. The Satanic Temple currently has over 20 chapters in the USA, in states like California, New York, Texas, and sadly (again) in my State of Michigan. So not only has faith in our God been dwindling in this nation, but Satanism is filling the void. The Holy Bible is clear that, in the Last Days, society will depart from the LORD and be "led astray" by fables - witchcraft - sorcery - false gods - and doctrines of demons. We are no doubt seeing all of these prophecies come to pass before our eyes, in a generation that knoweth not God.

While that sad realization would bring an end to this book, it would be irresponsible of me (as an ambassador for the LORD) to leave you without hope for change. While the world appears to be in the worst shape spiritually that it's ever been in, since Christ ascended into Heaven, what can we believers possibly do to turn the tide? Number one: Keep preaching God's Word and standing up for His truth in a world filled with Satan's lies. Number two: Train up your children to know the Lord. That way, when they go out on their own into this Godless society, they will draw closer to Him - as opposed to pull away. Number three: Make the Holy Bible available to *everyone.*

I suspect the reason so many people mock, criticize, or attack the Bible is because (as studies I have shared revealed) they have obviously never read it in the first place. This is what inspired me to head to my local dollar store one day and buy a couple dozen Bibles. I believe that until a majority of homes in America have a Bible in them, things can never get any better. Whenever I am at my day job, or in a particular place besides home for an extended period of time, I place a box of Bibles on my car or somewhere nearby with heavy foot traffic. I write the invitation on the box to "Please TAKE ONE." I've done this for a while now, and I hope that my idea will catch on and become a habit for other believers.

I don't think that people truly hate God. They just don't know Him. If given the chance to get to know Him, I think most would be inclined to want to do so. The problem is, in a society where belief in God and the Bible is becoming more and more frowned upon, most people won't purposely head out to purchase the Holy Book. Sadly, most of the younger generation avoid church at all costs. So, how then do we reach the "least Christian generation in American history"? We must get God's Word into their hands.

Yes, there are street evangelists who preach, and others who hand out Bible tracts, but most teenagers tend to avoid them. By leaving the Bibles out in the open with no one forcing it on them, I believe they'll be more inclined to take one. This way, it is only between them and God. No one else has to know that they took a Bible. This is especially important for youngsters reared in atheist homes, who'd never be allowed to purchase the Bible. Lord Jesus commanded us to take the Gospel to *all* creation, not just to other believers. We must take God's Word to *everyone*. By distributing free Bibles, you are planting a seed for everyone around you to be able to know God.

Most dollar stores sell Bibles, and I am sure everyone reading this should be able to spare at least five dollars to do God's Work. As I believe that the signs of our times are pointing to the Rapture in our generation, we should strive to get as many souls up there with us as we can. The unfortunate souls that are left behind are going to endure the worst tribulation that this world has ever seen. I sure don't want to be responsible for anyone going through that, because of me not doing my part to tell them about our Lord.

I'm issuing a call to my brothers and sisters in Christ who are fed up with the absence of God in this world, and in the hearts of its people - *put God's Word into their hands.* Buy 3, 7, 10, 12, or even 20 Bibles. Place them in public where unbelievers can easily find them. You may never meet those who accept your gifts, but know that every soul whom your Bible reaches will reach another - and another - and another - and so on and so on. Maybe they will start leaving Bibles for others to find! Can you imagine the chain reaction across America, and revival that could be sparked, by making the Bible as available to people as a daily newspaper?

This nation desperately needs the Word of God more so than ever before in our history; and if we don't give it to America, then who will? I say we start giving it freely right now, one Bible at a time - to one soul at a time. I believe that if we would all do this, we can change one neighborhood at a time - one town at a time - one city at a time - one county at a time - and one State at a time - until this country again becomes "One Nation under God" *all the time*. I pray this book has proven to you that Jesus is truly coming back soon. Do not be caught sleeping on the job when He arrives. Time is running out, so we believers must GET TO WORK. The King is coming! Our King is coming! Keep looking up.

THE FOOL HATH SAID IN HIS HEART, THERE IS NO GOD.

- PSALMS 14:1 & 53:1

ACKNOWLEDGMENTS

TO THE BENHAM BROTHERS - you two are the most genuine, humble, and kind souls I've ever known. When you had become household names, after being fired from HGTV because of your faith, I was immediately drawn to your mutually bold spirits for God. Everything you've preached, stood for, and written, is on the same page with my beliefs. Even when making the rounds on just about every news network, to tell the story of not sacrificing your faith for a hit TV show, you still took the time to respond to my messages. I have never known anyone else in the spotlight that's ever been as warm and approachable as you guys. You are both perfect examples of humility.

When I was still an amateur writer (at best), and my website was still just a blog with a couple hundred visitors, you'd granted me an interview to post there. Since then, you have always taken time out of your very busy schedules to be a part of the annual Christmas Special every year. On top of that, you have blessed me with the honor of being able to share your articles on the website. I believe the LORD has truly blessed the website, and has taken it to heights I'd never dreamed possible. I also believe that it would not have come as far as it has, in just a few short years, without your constant presence on it.

Though we've never met in person, you guys are like family to me. Definitely brothers from another mother! While I'd always been bold for our Lord since I began my walk with Him, because of the great mercy He had shown this poor sinner when He saved me, you have been the only guys who've *increased* that boldness and inspired me to take an even stronger stand for Him each new day. The way you live your lives, lead your families, and run your business, is an inspiration. Your Bible studies have taught me so many valuable lessons, and have revealed new truths that I'd yet to discover on my own. I believe the LORD brought you two into my life for a reason, and I will eternally be thankful that He did.

Jason, you've always taken the time to sit down and respond to every email that I've ever sent your way. Whether it be for an interview request, guidance, prayer, or just to get your opinion on an article for the website, you've always been there. You are more of a blessing than you'll ever know. You're the man brother.

David, I haven't always reached out to you as much as I have your brother; but whenever I have, just like him, you have always responded. Your contributions to the website and your advice are always appreciated so much. I am so glad that I finally get to tell the whole world just how #Ossum the Benham Brothers truly are.

May God bless you and yours always Bros.

NOTES

Chapter One: Anti-Semitism

1. "BDS IS NOTHING BUT BS": Anti-Israel Movement Fueling Anti-Semitism in Colleges," BiblicalSigns.com, September 6, 2016, https://biblicalsignsintheheadlines.com/2016/09/06/bds-is-nothing-but-bs-anti-israel-movement-fueling-anti-semitism-in-colleges/

2. "DEFEND THE JEWS: We Must NEVER FORGET the Holocaust," BiblicalSigns.com, January 27, 2017, https://biblicalsignsintheheadlines.com/2017/01/27/defend-the-jews-we-must-never-forget-the-holocaust/

Chapter Two: Christian Persecution

1. "50 MOST DANGEROUS COUNTRIES FOR CHRISTIANS: Over 200 Million Experience 'High-Level' Persecution," BiblicalSigns.com, January 12, 2018, https://biblicalsignsintheheadlines.com/2018/01/12/50-most-dangerous-countries-for-christians-over-200-million-experience-high-level-persecution/

2. "WORST YEAR YET: Global Persecution of Christians Hits Another All-Time High," BiblicalSigns.com, November 15, 2017, https://biblicalsignsintheheadlines.com/2017/11/15/worst-year-yet-global-persecution-of-christians-hits-another-all-time-high/

3. "MARTYRED EVERY 6 MINUTES: Christians Were Most Persecuted Group in 2016," BiblicalSigns.com, January 3, 2017, https://biblicalsignsintheheadlines.com/2017/01/03/martyred-every-6-minutes-christians-were-most-persecuted-group-in-2016/

4. "COPTIC CRISIS CONTINUES: Christian Persecution in Egypt Escalates," BiblicalSigns.com, June 21, 2016, https://biblicalsignsintheheadlines.com/2016/06/21/coptic-crisis-continues-christian-persecution-in-egypt-escalates/

5. "EGYPT'S EXTERMINATION OF CHRISTIANS CONTINUES: Islamists Massacre Nearly 30 More Coptic Christians," BiblicalSigns.com, May 27, 2017, https://biblicalsignsintheheadlines.com/2017/05/27/egypts-extermination-of-christians-continues-islamists-massacre-nearly-30-more-coptic-christians/

6. "BIBLE BAN: China's Crackdown on Christianity Continues as Word of God Pulled from All Online Retailers," BiblicalSigns.com, April 13, 2018, https://biblicalsignsintheheadlines.com/2018/04/13/bible-ban-chinas-crackdown-on-christianity-continues-as-word-of-god-pulled-from-all-online-retailers/

7. "LIBERAL HYPOCRISY: Kneeling in Prayer is Ridiculed, But Kneeling in Protest is Revered," BiblicalSigns.com, October 1, 2017, https://biblicalsignsintheheadlines.com/2017/10/01/liberal-hypocrisy-kneeling-in-prayer-is-ridiculed-but-kneeling-in-protest-is-revered/

8. "WE CAN'T BAKE THE CAKE: Why Christians Refuse to Participate in Gay Weddings," BiblicalSigns.com, February 9, 2018, https://biblicalsignsintheheadlines.com/2018/02/09/we-cant-bake-the-cake-why-christians-refuse-to-participate-in-gay-weddings/

9. "LGBT WAR ON CHRISTIANS RAMPS UP: How We Can Fight Back," BiblicalSigns.com, March 30, 2016, https://biblicalsignsintheheadlines.com/2016/03/30/lgbt-war-on-christians-ramps-up-how-we-can-fight-back/

10. "LGBT MAFIA TARGETS ANOTHER PAIR OF CHRISTIANS ON HGTV: It's Time for Believers to Turn the Tables," BiblicalSigns.com, December 1, 2016, https://biblicalsignsintheheadlines.com/2016/12/01/lgbt-mafia-targets-another-pair-of-christians-on-hgtv-its-time-for-believers-to-turn-the-tables/

11. "COLLEGES PURGING CHRISTIANITY: Secular Universities Kicking Out Christians in Name of Inclusiveness," BiblicalSigns.com, March 16, 2018, https://biblicalsignsintheheadlines.com/2018/03/16/colleges-purging-christianity-secular-universities-kicking-out-christians-in-name-of-inclusiveness/

12. "IMMORAL INSTITUTIONS: Public Schools Persecuting, Sullying and Alienating Christians," BiblicalSigns.com, April 21, 2017, https://biblicalsignsintheheadlines.com/2017/04/21/immoral-institutions-public-schools-persecuting-sullying-and-alienating-christians/

13. "CANADA'S WAR ON CHRISTIANS: Holy Bible CENSORED, and Biblical Beliefs CRIMINALIZED," BiblicalSigns.com, June 16, 2017, https://biblicalsignsintheheadlines.com/2017/06/16/canadas-war-on-christians-holy-bible-censored-and-biblical-beliefs-criminalized/

CHAPTER THREE: TERRORISM

1. "AS THE DAYS OF NOAH WERE: Worldwide Terrorism Reaches ALL-TIME HIGH," BiblicalSigns.com, June 1, 2017, https://biblicalsignsintheheadlines.com/2017/06/01/as-the-days-of-noah-were-worldwide-terrorism-reaches-all-time-high/

2. "WE ARE NOT AT WAR WITH ISIS: WE ARE AT WAR WITH ISLAM," BiblicalSigns.com, July 15, 2016, https://biblicalsignsintheheadlines.com/2016/07/15/we-are-not-at-war-with-isis-we-are-at-war-with-islam/

3. "ISLAMIC TERROR IS ISLAM: The Quran Says So," BiblicalSigns.com, December 7, 2015, https://biblicalsignsintheheadlines.com/2015/12/07/islamic-terror-is-islam-the-quran-says-so/

4. "EXPOSING ISLAM: The Anti-GOD Religion," BiblicalSigns.com, October 30, 2015, https://biblicalsignsintheheadlines.com/2015/10/30/exposing-islam-the-anti-god-religion/

CHAPTER FOUR: THE FIG TREE

1. "THIS GENERATION?: 70th Anniversary of Israel's Rebirth Could Herald Christ's Return," BiblicalSigns.com, November 10, 2017, https://biblicalsignsintheheadlines.com/2017/11/10/this-generation-70th-anniversary-of-israels-rebirth-could-herald-christs-return

2. "MAY 14th, 1948: The REBIRTH of Israel," BiblicalSigns.com, May 11, 2016, https://biblicalsignsintheheadlines.com/2016/05/11/may-14th-1948-the-rebirth-of-israel/

3. "5777: YEAR OF THE RAPTURE?," BiblicalSigns.com, September 9, 2016, https://biblicalsignsintheheadlines.com/2016/09/09/5777-are-you-rapture-ready/

4. 1948 Math, http://www.alphanewsdaily.com/mathprophecy2.html

CHAPTER FIVE: JERUSALEM

1. "FINALLY!: Trump Keeps Promise to Move Embassy as He Recognizes Jerusalem as Israel's Capital," BiblicalSigns.com, December 7, 2017, https://biblicalsignsintheheadlines.com/2017/12/07/finally-trump-keeps-promise-to-move-embassy-as-he-recognizes-jerusalem-as-israels-capital/

2. "MIRACLE OF 1967: 50th Anniversary of Israel's Victory in Six Day War and Reunification of JERUSALEM," BiblicalSigns.com, June 6, 2017, https://biblicalsignsintheheadlines.com/2017/06/06/miracle-of-1967-50th-anniversary-of-israels-victory-in-six-day-war-and-reunification-of-jerusalem/

3. "IT'S TIME TO CALL OUT THE REAL "OCCUPIERS" IN THE MIDDLE EAST (And Israel Isn't One of Them)," BiblicalSigns.com, May 6, 2018, https://biblicalsignsintheheadlines.com/2018/05/06/its-time-to-call-out-the-real-occupiers-in-the-middle-east-and-israel-isnt-one-of-them/

4. "THE HISTORY OF JERUSALEM: Israel's Capital is An Eternal GOD-GIVEN Possession," BiblicalSigns.com, December 9, 2017, https://biblicalsignsintheheadlines.com/2017/12/09/the-history-of-jerusalem-israels-capital-is-an-eternal-god-given-possession/

CHAPTER SIX: THE ENEMIES OF ISRAEL

1. "NATIONS GATHERED AGAINST JERUSALEM: Anti-Israel Vote At UN Fulfills Biblical Prophecy," BiblicalSigns.com, December 22, 2017, https://biblicalsignsintheheadlines.com/2017/12/22/nations-gathered-against-jerusalem-anti-israel-vote-at-un-fulfills-biblical-prophecy/

2. "ALLIED AGAINST ISRAEL: Is the Gog-Magog War At the Door?," BiblicalSigns.com, February 14, 2018, https://biblicalsignsintheheadlines.com/2018/02/14/allied-against-israel-is-the-gog-magog-war-at-the-door/

3. "DEFUND THE UN: America Must Stop Financing United Nations' War On Israel," BiblicalSigns.com, March 25, 2017, https://biblicalsignsintheheadlines.com/2017/03/25/defund-the-un-america-must-stop-financing-united-nations-war-on-israel/

4. "UNITED NATIONS CONTENDING WITH GOD: Anti-Israel Resolution Rewrites History of Jerusalem," BiblicalSigns.com, October 13, 2016, https://biblicalsignsintheheadlines.com/2016/10/13/united-nations-contending-with-god-anti-israel-resolution-rewrites-history-of-jerusalem/

5. "LAST DAYS' ENEMIES OF ISRAEL ON THE MARCH," BiblicalSigns.com, October 28, 2015, https://biblicalsignsintheheadlines.com/2015/10/28/last-days-enemies-of-israel-on-the-march/

6. "THE MOST ANTI-ISRAEL PRESIDENT OF ALL-TIME," BiblicalSigns.com, November 1, 2015, https://biblicalsignsintheheadlines.com/2015/11/01/the-most-anti-israel-president-of-all-time/

7. "REAL 'FAKE NEWS'": As Palestinians Terrorized Israel, Lamestream News Media Portrayed Them As VICTIMS,"

BiblicalSigns.com, May 17, 2018,
https://biblicalsignsintheheadlines.com/2018/05/17/real-fake-new
s-as-palestinians-terrorized-israel-lamestream-news-media-report
ed-exact-opposite/

CHAPTER SEVEN: SIGNS IN THE HEAVENS

1. "SIGNS IN THE HEAVENS CONTINUE: Supermoon Rises On
   Feast of Tabernacles," BiblicalSigns.com, October 16, 2016,
   https://biblicalsignsintheheadlines.com/2016/10/16/signs-in-the-h
   eavens-continue-supermoon-rises-on-feast-of-tabernacles/
2. "SUPERMOON OF THE CENTURY: Largest Moon Since
   Israel's Rebirth Rises Next Week," BiblicalSigns.com, November
   12, 2016,
   https://biblicalsignsintheheadlines.com/2016/11/12/supermoon-of-
   the-century-largest-moon-since-israels-rebirth-rises-next-week/
3. "WILL GOD DIVIDE AMERICA?: Once-In-A-Century Total
   Solar Eclipse Could Be A Final Warning," BiblicalSigns.com, June
   22, 2017,
   https://biblicalsignsintheheadlines.com/2017/06/22/will-god-divi
   de-america-once-in-a-century-total-solar-eclipse-could-be-a-final
   -warning/
4. "AMERICA'S ECLIPSE AND JERUSALEM: The Remarkable
   Connection Amplifies God's Warning," BiblicalSigns.com,
   August 18, 2017,
   https://biblicalsignsintheheadlines.com/2017/08/18/americas-ecli
   pse-and-jerusalem-the-remarkable-connection-amplifies-gods-wa
   rning/
5. "ONCE IN A BLUE SUPER BLOOD MOON,"
   BiblicalSigns.com, January 27, 2018,
   https://biblicalsignsintheheadlines.com/2018/01/27/once-in-a-blu
   e-super-blood-moon-rare-heavenly-event-has-not-occurred-in-ov
   er-150-years/
6. "MYSTERIOUS GLOBAL PHENOMENA IN THE HEAVENS,"
   BiblicalSigns.com, November 24, 2017,
   https://biblicalsignsintheheadlines.com/2017/11/24/mysterious-glo

bal-phenomena-in-the-heavens-loud-booms-and-trumpet-sounds
-baffle-scientific-community/

CHAPTER EIGHT: EARTHQUAKES & EXTREME WEATHER

1. "SIGN OF THE TIMES: Powerful Earthquakes,"
   BiblicalSigns.com, April 15, 2016,
   https://biblicalsignsintheheadlines.com/2016/04/15/sign-of-the-ti
   mes-powerful-earthquakes/

2. "MASSIVE EARTHQUAKE ON EVE OF HISTORIC
   SUPERMOON: 7.8 Magnitude Quake Strikes Near
   Christchurch, NZ," BiblicalSigns.com, November 13, 2016,
   https://biblicalsignsintheheadlines.com/2016/11/13/massive-earthq
   uake-on-eve-of-historic-supermoon-7-8-magnitude-quake-strikes
   -near-christchurch-new-zealand/

3. "AFTERSHOCKS: Looking Back At 2016's Powerful
   Earthquakes, And Looking Ahead To A BIG ONE in 2017,"
   BiblicalSigns.com, December 10, 2016,
   https://biblicalsignsintheheadlines.com/2016/12/10/aftershocks-lo
   oking-back-at-2016s-powerful-earthquakes-and-looking-ahead-to
   -a-big-one-in-2017/

4. "TRACKING THE TROPICS: Pay Close Attention To
   Biblically-Named Hurricanes," BiblicalSigns.com, May 25, 2018,
   https://biblicalsignsintheheadlines.com/2018/05/25/tracking-the-t
   ropics-pay-close-attention-to-biblically-named-hurricanes

5. "1st JUDGMENT FALLS: On Same Day Trump Renews
   Israeli-Palestinian Peace Push, U.S. Hurricane Forms,"
   BiblicalSigns.com, August 25, 2017,
   https://biblicalsignsintheheadlines.com/2017/08/25/1st-judgment-
   falls-on-same-day-trump-renews-israeli-palestinian-peace-push-u
   -s-hurricane-forms/

6. "2nd JUDGMENT: In Same Week of Trump's UNGA
   "Land-for-Peace" Push, Another Big Hurricane Targets USA,"
   BiblicalSigns.com, September 8, 2017,
   https://biblicalsignsintheheadlines.com/2017/09/08/2nd-judgmen
   t-in-same-week-of-trumps-unga-land-for-peace-push-another-big
   -hurricane-targets-usa/

7. "THE CASE AGAINST CLIMATE CHANGE: Combating the Theory That DENIES God," BiblicalSigns.com, May 10, 2017, https://biblicalsignsintheheadlines.com/2017/05/10/the-case-again st-climate-change-combating-the-theory-that-denies-god/

8. "GLOBAL WARMING? MORE LIKE GLOBAL COOLING: Who Can Withstand HIS Cold?," BiblicalSigns.com, January 19, 2018, https://biblicalsignsintheheadlines.com/2018/01/19/global-warmi ng-more-like-global-cooling-who-can-withstand-his-cold/

9. "UNNATURAL: Rare Weather Events Are Not Result of Climate Change, But Harbingers of Climactic Change," BiblicalSigns.com, April 20, 2018, https://biblicalsignsintheheadlines.com/2018/04/20/unnatural-rar e-weather-events-are-not-result-of-climate-change-but-harbinger s-of-climactic-change/

CHAPTER NINE: ABORTION

1. "DEFUND PLANNED PARENTHOOD: Over 7 Million Reasons Why It Must Be Done in 2018," BiblicalSigns.com, January 5, 2018, https://biblicalsignsintheheadlines.com/2018/01/05/defund-plann ed-parenthood-over-7-million-reasons-why-it-must-be-done-in-2 018/

2. "BENHAM BROS: "Sex Ed Sit Out" – Let's Take A Stand for Our Kids," BiblicalSigns.com, April 22, 2018, https://biblicalsignsintheheadlines.com/2018/04/22/benham-bros- sex-ed-sit-out-lets-take-a-stand-for-our-kids/

3. "AMERICA'S JUDGMENT COMING: Our Supreme Lawgiver Is Not A Court," BiblicalSigns.com, June 28, 2016, https://biblicalsignsintheheadlines.com/2016/06/28/judgment-co ming-our-supreme-authority-is-not-a-court/

CHAPTER TEN: LGBT PRIDE

1. "I STAND AGAINST PRIDE: Christians Cannot Stand With God AND the LGBT Movement (So Pick A Side),"

BiblicalSigns.com, June 10, 2017,
http://biblicalsignsintheheadlines.com/2017/06/10/i-stand-against
-pride-christians-cannot-stand-with-god-and-the-lgbt-movement
-so-pick-a-side/

2. "WE CAN'T BAKE THE CAKE: Why Christians Refuse To
Participate in Gay Weddings," BiblicalSigns.com, February 9,
2018,
http://biblicalsignsintheheadlines.com/2018/02/09/we-cant-bake-
the-cake-why-christians-refuse-to-participate-in-gay-weddings/

3. "TRANSGENDER INSANITY: God Created Male and Female ..
PERIOD," BiblicalSigns.com, July 4, 2017,
http://biblicalsignsintheheadlines.com/2017/07/04/transgender-in
sanity-god-created-male-and-female-period/

Chapter Eleven: Falling Away from the Faith

1. "FAITHLESS GENERATION: Belief in Holy Bible Dwindling,
Being Mocked, And Even Criminalized in America,"
BiblicalSigns.com, April 26, 2018,
https://biblicalsignsintheheadlines.com/2018/04/26/faithless-gene
ration-belief-in-holy-bible-dwindling-being-mocked-and-even-cr
iminalized-in-america/

2. "DISTURBING DISREGARD FOR THE TRUTH: Studies
Reveal Lack of Biblical Knowledge in America,"
BiblicalSigns.com, April 29, 2016,
https://biblicalsignsintheheadlines.com/2017/04/29/disturbing-di
sregard-for-the-truth-studies-reveal-americans-lack-of-biblical-k
nowledge/

3. "THE POPE'S LOVE AFFAIR WITH ISLAM: Is Francis
Revelation's "False Prophet"?," BiblicalSigns.com, August 1, 2016,
https://biblicalsignsintheheadlines.com/2016/08/01/the-popes-lov
e-affair-with-islam-is-francis-revelations-false-prophet/

4. "EMASCULATING THE LORD: Liberal Churches And Bible
Translators Adapt "Gender-Neutral" Pronouns for God,"
BiblicalSigns.com, December 2, 2017,
https://biblicalsignsintheheadlines.com/2017/12/02/emasculating-

the-lord-liberal-churches-and-bible-translators-adapt-gender-neu
tral-pronouns-for-god/

5. "GENDER-NEUTRAL NONSENSE: Episcopal Church of D.C.
   Will No Longer Acknowledge GOD As Masculine,"
   BiblicalSigns.com, February 1, 2018,
   https://biblicalsignsintheheadlines.com/2018/02/01/gender-neutra
   l-nonsense-episcopal-church-of-d-c-will-no-longer-acknowledge-
   god-as-masculine/

6. "SIN: The Word Nobody Wants To Hear, But SHOULD,"
   BiblicalSigns.com, November 10, 2015,
   https://biblicalsignsintheheadlines.com/2015/11/10/society-of-sin-
   why-stopping-it-starts-with-us/

Chapter Twelve: Faithless Generation

1. "DEGENERATION: New Study Finds "Generation Z" Is the
   Least Christian Generation in American History,"
   BiblicalSigns.com, January 25, 2018,
   https://biblicalsignsintheheadlines.com/2018/01/25/degeneration-
   new-study-finds-generation-z-is-the-least-christian-generation-in
   -american-history/

2. "FAITHLESS GENERATION: Belief in Holy Bible Dwindling,
   Being Mocked, and Even Criminalized in America,"
   BiblicalSigns.com, April 26, 2018,
   https://biblicalsigns.com/2018/04/26/faithless-generation-belief-i
   n-holy-bible-dwindling-being-mocked-and-even-criminalized-in-
   america/

3. "DOWNRIGHT DEMONIC DEMOCRATS: Town Hall
   Protesters Erupt in Anger At the Name of Jesus,"
   BiblicalSigns.com, February 28, 2017,
   https://biblicalsigns.com/2017/02/28/downright-demonic-democr
   ats-town-hall-protesters-erupt-in-anger-at-the-name-of-jesus/

4. "SATANIC WORSHIP ON THE RISE IN AMERICA,"
   BiblicalSigns.com, November 3, 2015,
   https://biblicalsignsintheheadlines.com/2015/11/03/satanic-worshi
   p-on-the-rise-in-america/

ABOUT THE AUTHOR

MICHAEL SAWDY is founder of the website *Biblical Signs in the Headlines*. He had a life-changing experience with Jesus Christ in 2006, which led him to turn from a sinful life and to dedicate his life to God. Since then, he has spent thousands of hours studying the Holy Bible - along with teachings by his greatest influences: Jason and David Benham, Jack Van Impe, Billy Graham, Chuck Missler, and John Hagee.

Due to the message he had received from the Lord, during his salvation experience, MichaEL believes that Jesus Christ is truly coming back *soon*. This belief is what sparked an interest in "Last Days" Bible Prophecy, specifically concerning the Rapture of the Church. In 2014, he began writing about global events, which had mirrored Biblical prophecies, for the Christian news outlet known as *The Truth Dispatch*.

In the Fall of 2015, he felt a calling by the Lord to create his own website, *BiblicalSigns.com*, to present news and views from a Biblical perspective. The website surpassed one-million visitors within just two years. After over a decade of Biblical study, and writing in-depth articles about the *signs of our times*, he felt that the Holy Spirit inspired him to write this book.

VISIT THE WEBSITE:
BiblicalSigns.com
FOLLOW ON SOCIAL MEDIA:
Facebook - /BiblicalSignsInTheHeadlines
Twitter - @MichaelofYHWH (Personal)
@BiblicalSigns (Website)
@SignsofTimes777 (Book)